POWER and PROMISE

Living your Life with Power fulfilling God's Promises on Purpose!

The Identity for Life Teaching Series

Book II

Wanda L. Scott

Foreword by Pastor Daniel Miree

Power and Promise
Living your Life with Power fulfilling God's Promises on Purpose

Copyright © 2016 Wanda L. Scott
Originally portions of this book were copyrighted in ©2006 as ***Identity Theft***: *Strengthening Our Youth Through the Grey Areas of Life*

All rights reserved. No part of this book may be reproduced or transmitted in any form or by any means, electronic or mechanical, including photocopying, recording or by any information storage and retrieval system, without written permission from the author, except for the inclusion of brief quotations in a review.

Unless otherwise noted, Scripture quotations are from the King James Version of the Bible.
Scripture quotations noted by NKJV are taken from the Holy Bible, New King James Version copyright © 1979, 1980, 1982 by Thomas Nelson, Inc.
Scripture quotations noted by RSV are taken from the Revised Standard Version of the Bible, copyright © 1946, 1952, and 1971 by the National Council of the Churches of Christ in the USA. Used by permission. All rights reserved.
Scripture quotations noted by AMP are from the Amplified Bible
Copyright © 2015 by The Lockman Foundation, La Habra, CA 90631. All rights reserved.
Scripture quotations noted by NLT are from the Holy Bible, New Living Translation, copyright © 1996, 2004, 2015 by Tyndale House Foundation. Used by permission of Tyndale House Publishers Inc., Carol Stream, Illinois 60188. All rights reserved.

Editor: Wanda J. S. Banks
Cover Design by Preston Spencer
Inside Layout and Design by Wanda L. Scott

ISBN 978-0-9761322-6-4 Paperback
ISBN 978-0-9761322-3-3   eBook

10 9 8 7 6 5 4 3 2 1

Published through the Image Institute
(A Division of WLS Enterprises)
www.Image-Institute.org

Printed in the Unites States of America

Wanda L. Scott

ACKNOWLEDGEMENTS

As I prepare to release this second book of what was originally the book *Identity Theft*, I am so excited about the reception of *Life and Love*! It has fueled my passion and faith in the Lord that the release of these two books, *Life and Love* and *Power and Promise*, is divine. I know these books are an instructional part of what God is doing and saying in this time and season. I am in awe of God and humbled that I can be a part of His move in the earth, as His kingdom comes and His will is done on earth as it is in heaven.

I want to acknowledge the divine hand of the Lord in connecting me with Pastor Daniel Miree and the STBF church who are building and believing to see the Power and Promise of God here on earth as it is in heaven. I pray God's continued hand of blessing, power, provision and promotion on this body of believers as God uses them mightily for the kingdom of God.

I also want to thank my mother who has faithfully read and re-read and edited my books. Her selfless support and belief in me has given me encouragement to keep writing knowing she is with me and helping me when no one else is. I love her dearly.

For these two books God sent a ram in the bush for me with my graphics designer Preston Spencer. His covers for these two books came from divine inspiration and his generosity enabled me to move forward and publish these books on God's schedule. I thank him for his time and diligence in meeting my deadlines. I could not have pictured the covers in my mind any better!

As always I am thankful to the Lord God and the power of the Holy Spirit that empowers me to write and share God's Word in this form.

Wanda L. Scott

TABLE OF CONTENTS

ACKNOWLEDGEMENTS 4
INTRODUCTION 7
FOREWORD 11
CHAPTER 1: LIFE WITH JESUS 15
    DECLARATIONS 24
CHAPTER 2: SOMETHING ABOUT THAT NAME 26
    DECLARATIONS 40
CHAPTER 3: GOD'S POWER PERSONIFIED 43
    DECLARATIONS 56
CHAPTER 4: HOW TO DEFINE SUCCESS 59
    DECLARATIONS 71
CHAPTER 5: GROWING BEYOND PLAYING CHURCH 73
    DECLARATIONS 90
Bibliography 96
Scripture References 97

A Note from the Author…….

These books have really been a journey looking back at my life's path until now. What does it mean to accept the Lord at 7 years old, and how does a child process that pull from God to accept Jesus. What were my next steps, influences, and how was Christ-likeness modeled before me? These questions led me to seek out God's Word and how He wants these questions answered in order to live a life pleasing to God day by day & to raise children in His image and likeness. I am so blessed that the Lord has kept me and allowed me to make it through the wrong choices in the grey areas, and by His mercy live to try and make the right choices in the grey areas. We all have a path to take, lessons to be learned, and opportunities to see God in it each and every time. I hope that this book will help those coming behind me and those on their present journey to keep their eyes focused on not only God's mercy, love and grace, but also on God's will for each of our lives. It is only in seeing, fearing, loving and yielding to Christ that we will truly learn our own identity, thus being a part of the kingdom of God helping His will to be done and His kingdom to come here on earth as it is in heaven.

Thank you God for your Holy Spirit and the gifting and anointing you have placed on my life. May the grace of the Lord Jesus Christ, and the love of God, and the communion of the Holy Spirit *be* with you. Amen.

Working Every Day to Walk in His Will,
Wanda L. Scott

INTRODUCTION

The *Identity for Life* Teaching Series of books lays out for us the scripture that feeds us the fundamentals of our God-identity. Each book shows us how the Word of God applies to our everyday living, walking in love toward God and others. There is a specific focus on personal accountability by agreeing with God's Word, and our responsibility to those we come in contact with every day. As we move into this second (2nd) book in this series, it is important that we remind ourselves of the 21 Identity Principles from Life and Love. God's Word is our firm foundation, so we need to confess and agree with these one more time before we move into additional building of our spiritual house.

21 Identity Principles
Life and Love: For Life & Love you have to know what you are in Agreement with!

Identity Principle #1
God does not just design our exterior uniqueness, but He fashions our lives to make our intrinsic character, which defines our soul and spirit.
Ephesians 2:10; Philippians 1:6; Galatians 5:22-26; Romans 12:1-2
©2015 Life and Love www.WandaLScott.com

Identity Principle #2
When we identify with another person or thing we begin to take on characteristics similar to it.
Romans 6:16; Romans 12:1-2
©2015 Life and Love www.WandaLScott.com

Identity Principle #3
We must live a life pleasing to God, so that our children will know what that type of godly life looks like.
Deuteronomy 11:18-21; Romans 12:2; James 1:25
©2015 Life and Love www.WandaLScott.com

Identity Principle #4
Our children need to see the love of God in action through us helping others and giving of ourselves.
James 1:27; Malachi 3:5; 1 John 4:11
©2015 Life and Love www.WandaLScott.com

Identity Principle #5
If we know our identity, we know we find it in the Word of God.
Genesis 1:26; 1 John 2:15-17; Ephesians 2:1-3;
©2015 Life and Love www.WandaLScott.com

Identity Principle #6
To be a child of God we are accepting Jesus Christ as our Lord and Savior.
Galatians 3:26;1 John 3:1; 5:1;John 1:12
©2015 Life and Love www.WandaLScott.com

Identity Principle #7
Walking in the Spirit is living according to the "teachings of the bible" by the power of the Holy Spirit.
1 John 3:10; 5:2; Galatians 2:20; 5:22-23
©2015 Life and Love www.WandaLScott.com

Identity Principle #8
We are not to live according to our own will obeying our flesh.
2 Corinthians 13:15-16; John 16:33; Galatians 2:20; 5:22-23
©2015 Life and Love www.WandaLScott.com

Identity Principle #9
We are saved through faith in Jesus Christ, not by anything we can do.
Ephesians 2:8-10; Hebrews 7:25
©2015 Life and Love www.WandaLScott.com

Identity Principle #10
We are commanded to love and we are responsible to pass this love on to our children as we are compelled by the overwhelming love of God toward us.
Luke 10:27; 1 Thess. 3:12;
©2015 Life and Love www.WandaLScott.com

Wanda L. Scott

Identity Principle #11

God's love is a love that we can only consistently show through intimacy in our relationship with Jesus & the guidance of the Holy Spirit.

2 Peter 1:5-9;1 John 4:16-19
©2015 Life and Love www.WandaLScott.com

Identity Principle #12

No attack of the enemy or tragedy in this world can take our life or ultimately destroy us if we trust & believe in God.

Isaiah 54:17; 2 Corinthians 4:8-10
©2015 Life and Love www.WandaLScott.com

Identity Principle #13

When we just accept any spirit we are open to such things as witchcraft, sorcery, and fleshy sinful behavior.

Romans 8:16; John 16:13; Leviticus 20:6;
©2015 Life and Love www.WandaLScott.com

Identity Principle #14

The Word says in spirit and in truth; the spirit comes first because there is no way you can see the truth without the Holy Spirit.

John 15:26; John 4:23; John 1:17; John 8:32
©2015 Life and Love www.WandaLScott.com

Identity Principle #15

What we do every day, how we respond to situations, and what we speak out of our mouths testify to the Jesus in us.

1 Peter 1:17-23; John 14:17; John 8:44
©2015 Life and Love www.WandaLScott.com

Identity Principle #16

When we are intoxicated with anything else but the Holy Spirit, we can be blocked from hearing God clearly. This can cause us to stray out of God's will.

Isaiah 28:7-8; Galatians 5:16; Acts 6:3
©2015 Life and Love www.WandaLScott.com

Identity Principle #17
The devil is very smart. He thinks if I can get them drunk, then it will be even harder for them to resist temptation and obey God.
Proverbs 23:29-35; Ephesians 5:14-20
©2015 Life and Love www.WandaLScott.com

Identity Principle #18
Being part of the body of Christ changes our every decision and action. If we are the body, then we don't make our own decisions anymore.
1 Corinthians 12:12-14; 1 Corinthians 1:10; 2:16; Philippians 2:5
©2015 Life and Love www.WandaLScott.com

Identity Principle #19
We should be striving to walk in Harmony and as a good example to one another, teaching and cautioning one another to do what is right in God's eyes.
Titus 2:1-8; Colossians 3:16; Ephesians 4:15-17
©2015 Life and Love www.WandaLScott.com

Identity Principle #20
We must sincerely seek the Lord on every relationship we participate in, including the familial relationships that we inherit in Christ.
1 Corinthians 3:1-3; 2 Corinthians 10:3-4; Romans 8:6-8
©2015 Life and Love www.WandaLScott.com

Identity Principle #21
If we are serving the true and living God, we will be able to worship Him in Spirit and in truth regardless of what color or culture is represented when we are in fellowship with one another.
Ephesians 6:10-12; Galatians 3:28; Colossians 3:10-11
©2015 Life and Love www.WandaLScott.com

Wanda L. Scott

FOREWORD

To say how amazing and timely God is would of course be an understatement. It's a wonderful joy to experience how strategic God has connected the body of Christ. Wanda L. Scott is indeed a blessing to the body of Christ, whom for me represents a symbiotic connection in the spirit. She articulates a kingdom perspective that is long overdue for the Christian development. The heart of God's people now focuses on the purity of God's authority, power, and nature through His children. Wanda Scott's WISDOM and PRACTICAL application through the spirit of the Lord draws Christians away from tradition and into a real relationship. I stand in awe of how the insight disseminated throughout kingdom minded leaders is lining up almost verbatim. After several conversations with Wanda L. Scott, we quickly found common spiritual ground that joined us together for a kingdom agenda. Upon planting a new work in the greater Nashville area, I began teaching an aggressive message of supernatural giftings for today's maturing believer. After reading "Power and Promise", I was floored how the same principals were being uncovered expansively! If you've ever had a moment where you knew God affirmed His revelation to you through the voice of another believer, you understand how I felt reading it.

With so many self-help books to choose from in our healthy diet of Christian reading, Wanda Scott stands out for two reasons. First, the material covers a vast region of introspective reflection accompanied by reader involvement. This is not just an informative work, but also a collaborative effort on the behalf of anyone who takes serious their journey to a deeper revelation. Secondly, this book is not designed to make a profit (although I'm sure she wants it to be a Best Seller); moreover her heart is to raise kingdom awareness for the King. The seeds she sows will shift the ordinary narrative of Christian identity and functionality. As a follow up to the first book, Wanda takes us deeper still, to the core of grasping a holistic view of the power God invests in each believer and their connection to purpose in this life.

Any leader who displays their truth is worth following. Wanda Scott's personal testimony affirms this book in practice. Her steps of faith to take the journey away from a 9 to 5, suggests she knows the power of God and the purpose He has laid out for her. Her character has been exemplary and consistent since I've known her. Plus, she's just an old fashioned kind of smart. God has truly blessed this child of God with a dynamic voice for years to come. Her legacy is establishing generations of Kingdom Builders, who will soon admire a brilliant mind in Wanda L. Scott.

Elder Daniel Miree, Executive Pastor
Spirit & Truth Believer's Fellowship
Nashville, TN

POWER and PROMISE

1
LIFE WITH JESUS

John 10^{10} *The thief comes only to steal and kill and destroy; I came that they may have life, and have it abundantly. (NRSV)*

IN THE FIRST BOOK, *LIFE AND LOVE,* we learned about being a child of God. This means that we identify ourselves with Jesus and agree with who and what He says we are. God's word gives us peace in our salvation. We must prepare ourselves to not only be servants of God, but also to be a witness by walking in faith. As we do these things we are living our life with Jesus. This life with Jesus manifests through growing in our personal relationship with Him. Our faith grows by hearing the Word of God (Romans 10:17). As we spend personal time getting to know Jesus in the Word of God, our faith grows even more. As we grow, we must guard our hearts and minds, so they will stay secure in our faith. This is the faith that points us to our identity in Jesus Christ.

> Be anxious for nothing, but in everything by prayer and supplication, with thanksgiving, let your requests be made known to God; and the peace of God, which surpasses all understanding, will guard your hearts and minds through Christ Jesus (Philippians 4:6-7).
>
> Watch, stand fast in the faith, be brave, be strong. Let all that you do be done with love (1 Corinthians 16:13-14).

The Word gives us strength to stand in faith, looking forward to the abundant life God says we can have. This abundant life manifests as we agree with God's word, resting in His love. The world's message we have to guard our hearts against beckons us to fall, not stand.

POWER and PROMISE

The world's message to us and our children is one of inclusion, assimilation, and a value system based on self-fulfillment. We have to live in this world, not immerse ourselves and do everything that it has to offer. Every day we either send our children out into the world or they go with us about our daily chores. We can be immersed in the things of the world just by turning on the TV. So how do we combat this onslaught of information that we are exposed to daily that does not always agree with the Word of God? We have to constantly be mindful of our surroundings and the situations we put ourselves into. Our efforts to stay in the Word of God through options such as reading the Bible or listening to gospel music that ministers the truth, have to be intentional in our day to day activities. When Paul writes to the church of Ephesus he warns them to: *See then that ye walk circumspectly, not as fools, but as wise, redeeming the time, because the days are evil. Wherefore be ye not unwise, but understanding what the will of the Lord is (Ephesians 5:15-17 NRSV).* The bible says to meditate on God's Word day and night, and literally this is what we have to do to keep our minds clear of the negative and misleading messages the world can send us all day. The devil is the "prince of the power of the air", and utilizes radio, television, and all forms of communication to tempt and manipulate our minds off of the Truth of God. When Joshua took over after Moses died, the Lord encouraged him with these Words:

> This book of the law shall not depart out of thy mouth; but thou shalt meditate therein day and night, that thou mayest observe to do according to all that is written therein: for then thou shalt make thy way prosperous, and then thou shalt have good success. (Joshua 1:8)

God has given us the solution to our question of 'How To' combat these misleading messages that contradict the Word of God; we now have to mindfully carryout the mandate of keeping our minds on the guidance in the Word and not the temptations of the world. This is how we have life with Jesus, abundant life.

Wanda L. Scott

Identity Principle

We have to live in this world, but we don't have to do everything that it has to offer.

Inclusion

Inclusion is subtly taught to our children as they enter the world alone. There are rules to follow on the bus, in school, and in any organized gathering that they are told to follow. In doing this they are taught to act according to the rules so they can be included and not punished in some way. This causes them to behave or act the same way others do. They form habits through learned behavior. Why is this a bad thing, you ask? Well in some ways it is not because it does teach discipline and respect for authority, but in other ways it could be harmful if the children do not have a firm foundation at home to balance the learned behavior of becoming a follower. Following rules is necessary as we are taught to follow God's commandments. But what happens when our children are faced with being told to follow the rules of a person who is not of God, or is abusing their authority. Or when following the rules means following the popular kids? Following can put your child into a situation where they are in mental or physical danger. This form of inclusion is the trickery the enemy uses to influence us into harmful and destructive situations. This falls back on our home life, teaching our children and giving them a firm foundation which is in Jesus Christ. If we have taught, and are teaching our children God's ways and principles, then when the world tells them something misleading and harmful, they will understand the difference. The world wants us to be followers so we can feel like we need to be included in all that it offers; when what it offers is death not life. The life we live is in Jesus

> We must teach our children so they will have discernment in these situations.

Christ. We must teach our children so they will have discernment in these situations so they can follow the rules, but not follow the world. Life as a child of God looks different from the world. Life with Jesus requires separation because we are set-apart, the way we do life is not like everyone else.

> And in accordance with this will [of God] we [who believe in the message of salvation] have been sanctified [that is, set apart as holy for God and His purposes] through the offering of the body of Jesus Christ (the Messiah, the Anointed) once for all. (Hebrews 10:10 AMP)

Assimilation

Once a child is in the world, he or she will feel the need to be assimilated. Assimilation is a step further than inclusion, as it means that the child will conform or blend in to the culture of the world. Webster defines assimilation as, *to make similar; to make into like substance; or absorb into the system.* We as children of God are called out of the world, sanctified, or 'set apart'. God calls us peculiar people, so the only 'like substance' we should be is 'like Jesus'. Assimilation is contrary to the way the Lord instructs us to behave to be acceptable in His sight, living by His Word. From the very beginning, God instructed Moses to warn the Israelites not to intermingle with or marry the inhabitants of the heathen nations they would conquer and occupy. God knew the power and persuasion the world would have on mankind; the spirit is willing, but the flesh is weak.

> Watch and pray that ye enter not into temptation: the spirit indeed is willing, but the flesh is weak. (Matthew 26:41)

The flesh is weak whether we are old or young. This causes us to be susceptible to the "pleasures" of the world. When we are encouraged to be assimilated in any way, such as friendships or any type of relationship, there is the possibility of being persuaded to conform to practices or habits of those we have assimilated with. In the book of Exodus chapter 34, Moses was instructed by God to warn the people of being in covenant with the inhabitants of the conquered lands. Being in covenant means any binding agreement, such as marriage in today's world. In the world today we enter into covenant through co-habitation, fornication, male-female relationships, and many other relational forms. In this way we begin to assimilate to each other's behavior; that is the primary reason that God warns us to not be unequally yoked in relationships (2 Corinth 6:14).

Identity Principle

The flesh is weak whether we are old or young!

Here is what God spoke to the Israelites in Exodus on the subject of assimilation:
> Take heed to yourself, lest you make a covenant with the inhabitants of the land whither you go, lest it become a snare in the midst of you. You shall tear down their altars, and break their pillars, and cut down their Ashe'rim (for you shall worship no other god, for the LORD, whose name is Jealous, is a jealous God), lest you make a covenant with the inhabitants of the land, and when they play the harlot after their gods and sacrifice to their gods and one invites you, you eat of his sacrifice, and you take of their daughters for your sons, and their daughters play the harlot after their gods and make your sons play the harlot after their gods. (Exodus 34:12-16)

This is the pattern in which we in the flesh can be persuaded to assimilate in any covenant or relational situation. Think about your last relationship. Whether it was a good male or female friendship or dating relationship, did you come out of it with any of their sayings, habits or behaviors. If you are still in the relationship, I bet you can see at least one way they have changed you. I don't believe that the Lord is implying that you cannot be of some type of godly influence, but our flesh has an inherit sin nature and is more inclined to go the easy way of sin, than to go with the disciplined life of Christ. That is why we have the indwelling Holy Spirit to guide us. This guidance provides conviction and a hunger for the Word of God. With the Holy Spirit's guidance we have a life of covenant with God. Any other covenant relationship has to be secondary, and in line with the will of God. This assures us of a consistent and rewarding life with Jesus by faith.

Self-Fulfillment

> Do not love the world or the things in the world. If anyone loves the world, love for the Father is not in him. For all that is in the world, the lust of the flesh and the lust of the eyes and the pride of life, is not of the Father but is of the world. And the world passes away, and the lust of it; but he who does the will of God abides forever. (1 John 2:15-17 NRSV)

The world entices us to lust after anything our flesh desires. One way we satisfy the flesh is by fulfilling our selfish needs. This is the behavior promoted in the world. The world teaches us to value ourselves through self-fulfillment regardless of others needs or feelings. This is exactly contrary to God's first and greatest commandment; love God with all your heart, soul, and mind, and love your neighbor as you love yourself. Therefore we are to think of our neighbors just as much as we are to think of ourselves. In 1 Corinthians 10:24 we see that we are responsible for each other's well-being. There are numerous other commands that state that we should care for orphans, widows, and those less fortunate (the needy) than ourselves out of the blessings we have been afforded. So we cannot take on the values of self-fulfillment that the world tries to impose on us or our children. We have to teach them the true Spirit of God, and have them walk in it in order to combat the selfish nature of this world. We are blessed to be a blessing. This is part of the abundant life.

This selfish spirit has opened the door for the enemy to convince the world that anything they imagine in their heart is acceptable. We see in Genesis 6:5 that our hearts are evil with vain imagination already, so the more the world encourages us to cater to ourselves and our inherent sinful nature, we instinctly follow. *Then the LORD saw that the wickedness of man was great in the earth, and that every intent of the thoughts of his heart was only evil continually* (Genesis 6:5 NKJV). This spirit of selfishness makes it even harder for man to come to the Lord when they are used to living free to do as they please, even though it is ultimately hurting them and others. If we leave our young people alone to figure life out on their own, they will take on what they see and hear every day. The way of the world is enticing and our human nature wants to succumb to the flesh. Therefore, in fulfilling selfish desires, our children will willingly follow the world.

> The world pushes inclusion, assimilation, and a value system based on self-fulfillment

Identity Principle

Self-fulfillment should not be a characteristic of the child of God. The Spirit of God in us will help us combat the selfish nature of our flesh.

The Grey Area

Inclusion, assimilation, and a value system based on self-fulfillment have saturated the world, and will consume us and our children in an effort to simultaneously steal our true identities from us. This identity in Christ is key to our life with Him. We are armed with the Word of God to give us practical examples and application to equip us with what we need to stop this ungodly influence. We have to hold ourselves accountable. We have to agree with what God says about us, what we do, and how we live. This accountability is not just for us, but for the younger generation, so we can step up and be proactive to every attack of the devil. As we read God's Word we can identify evil patterns and approaches that entice and tempt us. Knowledge of God's Word is the key to maintaining our faith walk with Him through Jesus Christ. This knowledge is for life.

We have all been under attack by temptations in one form or another if we are a child of God. Those moments were our grey areas where we had to make a choice. We must use our testimony and other experiences where God has brought us out, to be an example to new believers and those coming after us. Solomon, the wise king, let us know that "there is nothing new under the sun". We must swallow our pride and let our children know that we have been there in battle with the world and the lust of it, so that they will know that they don't have to stand alone. The bible says that we are saved by the blood of the Lamb, and the Word of our testimony (Rev. 12:7). We have to let our children know that Jesus stood alone for us, so that we do not have to. Life with Jesus means that we will never be alone. Agreement with God's word provides wisdom for a life that will be proactive and will testify of His power over temptation. God's Holy Spirit and the truth of His Word will give us strength in the grey areas.

> **We have all been under attack by temptations in one form or another if we are a child of God.**

Identity Principle

We have to hold ourselves accountable.
As we read God's Word we can identify evil desires and tendencies that tempt us.

Wanda L. Scott

Who is watching our children?
to keep them from the thief
who comes but to steal, kill and destroy?

Who is teaching our children?
to help them learn the things
that will keep them safe forever more?

We must guide our children
in the ways of the Lord.
We must protect our children
by showing them Jesus Christ and heaven's eternal door.

WLS

DECLARATION: *Repeat these out loud...and then answer the question.*

1. ***I agree that I don't have to do everything the world has to offer me.*** Name one thing that you have turned away from by the power of God.

2. ***I agree that my flesh is weak no matter whether I am old or young, BUT God's Holy Spirit gives me power to overcome as I meditate on it day and night!***
   Name one way you have overcome.

3. ***I agree with God that I am to be "set apart" for His work & glory! I will not fall to inclusion, assimilation, and a value system based on self-fulfillment.***
   Have you seen any subtle pushes to be assimilated in your life?

Action for Abundant Life

AWARENESS: Do you believe that your relationships can affect your walk with God?   Can you give an example of when this has happened in your life?

AWARENESS: How have you been under attack with temptations in your life? Would you be willing to share that example with a child or a new Christian to encourage them on their journey with Christ?

UNDERSTANDING: Which Identity Principle in this chapter did you relate to the most?   Why?

2
SOMETHING ABOUT THAT NAME

Acts 4[18] *And they called them, and commanded them not to speak at all nor teach in the name of Jesus. (NRSV)*

There is power, power, wonder working power in the blood of the Lamb. There is power, power, wonder working power in the precious blood of the Lamb. – Lewis E. Jones

THESE ARE THE WORDS OF A SONG I GREW UP singing in church, but little did I know about the true power of the Lamb of God, Jesus Christ. There is no other name on earth, at which every knee shall bow and every tongue shall confess that Jesus Christ is Lord. Even as I type this I feel the love, the power, and the joy the Lord gives me each and every day. Jesus is our identity. Jesus is life, "new life" for all that confess of his sovereign resurrection power.

Jesus is the ultimate identity definer.

Identity Principle

Jesus provides us with the true identity that the world attempts to steal from us. Jesus is who we as children of God should strive to be like.

Jesus is the ultimate identity definer. He is who we all should strive to be as children of God. He is who the world does not want us to speak of. He is who the evil one, with his legion of fallen angels, spends all their time trying to steal our faith from. Jesus provides us with the true identity that the world attempts to steal from us.

In Acts 4:18 above, we see that "they" who represent the world, commanded the disciples (we as children of God) not to speak or teach in the name of Jesus. It is amazing that the world knows the power of the name of Jesus and seems to believe in it more than we do as children of God. This same thing is happening today as the world attempts to take every opportunity to remove God, and the mention of His name from every aspect of our lives. Local governments are threatening students with jail time if they speak about or give glory to God in educational ceremonies! No matter how hard the world tries, the earth will still be filled with the Glory of the Lord (Habakkuk 2:14). The leaders of the Jews saw the disciples speak boldly and with power. Watching them they knew that they had been with Jesus. Today others recognize the presence of the Lord in your life, even if they don't know the Lord, or exactly what it is about you; His light shines through you. We as God's children must begin to recognize and understand the power that we have in the Holy Ghost. Jesus has given us an amazing gift, a powerful ability to bring glory to God through His name. There is truly something about the name Jesus that is undeniable.

> Today others do still recognize the presence of the Lord in your life.

Our life with Jesus began when we were born again. Once we confessed faith in the Lord Jesus and believed it with a repentant heart, we were given the gift of the Holy Spirit and are provided with powers and abilities to be performed in the name of Jesus.

> Then Peter said unto them, Repent, and be baptized every one of you in the name of Jesus Christ for the remission of sins, and ye shall receive the gift of the Holy Ghost. (Acts 2:38)

> And these signs will follow those who believe: In My name they will cast out demons; they will speak with new tongues; they will take up serpents; and if they drink anything deadly, it will by no means hurt them; they will lay hands on the sick, and they will recover." (Mark 16:17-18 NKJV)

POWER and PROMISE

These signs and miracles will be and can be seen either instantly, or as we become more like Jesus and learn to walk in God's will. As a follower of Jesus Christ we have certain promises that we should exercise in agreement with God's Word. We learn these things and are given power to walk in them by the Holy Spirit.

> But the Comforter, which is the Holy Ghost, whom the Father will send in my name, he shall teach you all things, and bring all things to your remembrance, whatsoever I have said unto you. (John 14:26)

We must rely on the power of God and His indwelling Holy Spirit to teach us our identity in Christ. We must be willing to subject ourselves to the teaching of the Holy Spirit as the Word of God is refined in us. We will shine as pure gold if we endure the trials we face in this world. As we hold on to the Lord by faith, He will guide us through. The process is not all full of pain and suffering. There are valleys, but there are also mountains. Mountain tops come when we have endured and become closer to the Lord, perfecting our worship and basking in His love. The continual love of Christ is enough to give us the strength to fight every battle the enemy wages against us.

> I will bring the one-third through the fire, will refine them as silver is refined, and test them as gold is tested. They will call on My name, and I will answer them. I will say, 'This is My people'; And each one will say, 'The LORD is my God.'" (Zechariah 13:9 NKJV)

As a child of God, we are identified with Christ, and the enemy who tried to steal God's glory from the beginning of time (Isaiah 14:12-21) will also try and steal your light, the light of the love of Jesus Christ. The world will try and load us down with its lies, in order to distract us from the truth of God. This distraction which is a trade ploy of the enemy is meant to lure us into things that our flesh can identify with, so as to pull us out of the Spirit. The flesh is easily distracted. We see in the Word that the Spirit is willing, but the flesh is week. The enemy knows this and will try every temptation possible to entice the flesh. But if we know the

Word of God, we know that the Lord will not allow us to be tempted with more than we can bare, and will always give us a way of escape (1 Corinthians 10:4). It is so imperative that we always turn to the Word for the truth when a lie is presented to us. That is why we must know how to seek truth in the Word as the Holy Spirit gives us wisdom. We must depend on the Holy Spirit for discernment when situations presented to us just don't seem right.

> And he said, "Beware that you are not led astray; for many will come in my name and say, 'I am he!' and, 'The time is near!' Do not go after them. (Luke 21:8 NRSV)

The devil is not only trying to steal our identity in Christ by tempting our flesh, but the bible also speaks of false prophets who come claiming Christ, but who are really teaching lies and deceit. In this situation we also must know the Word for ourselves, as not to be led astray by what sounds right or what sounds good. Men can have their own interpretations of the Word of God, but only the Holy Spirit can show us the revealed truth from God. Scripture taken out of context and pieced together can be twisted to make even the falsest religion sound holy.

Identity Principle

We should always turn to the Word for the truth when a lie is presented to us.

Identity on Purpose

We have not just been granted access into the family of God to say that we have membership. We are not a part of the body of Christ so we can just have a family. We have this identity in Jesus Christ so that we can serve Him in the kingdom of God, helping Him do His work here on earth. In serving God we serve one another in love and build the kingdom of God on earth as it is in heaven. In order to build the kingdom of God we each must individually bear fruit.

> Ye have not chosen me, but I have chosen you, and ordained you, that ye should go and bring forth fruit, and that your fruit should remain: that whatsoever ye shall ask of the Father in my name, he may give it to you. (John 15:16)

> Abide in Me, and I in you. As the branch cannot bear fruit of itself, unless it abides in the vine, neither can you, unless you abide in Me. "I am the vine, you are the branches. He who abides in Me, and I in him, bears much fruit; for without Me you can do nothing. If anyone does not abide in Me, he is cast out as a branch and is withered; and they gather them and throw them into the fire, and they are burned. If you abide in Me, and My Words abide in you, you will ask what you desire, and it shall be done for you. By this My Father is glorified, that you bear much fruit; so you will be My disciples. (John 15:4-8 NKJV)

> Therefore, my brethren, you also have become dead to the law through the body of Christ, that you may be married to another—to Him who was raised from the dead, that we should bear fruit to God. For when we were in the flesh, the sinful passions which were aroused by the law were at work in our members to bear fruit to death. (Romans 7:4-5 NKJV)

This is our mandate, to bear fruit in the kingdom of God. When we bear fruit it testifies to our connection to God. 'Fruit' is the manifestation of God's good works through us as His body in Christ. Some evidence of 'fruit' that will be noticed in you is the fruit of the Spirit (Galatians 5:22). Also in identifying with Jesus Christ we began to act on purpose. This is either being purposeful as a child of God fulfilling the Great Commission (Matthew 28:16-20), or being intentional in walking in God's revealed purpose for our individual life. In your private time with Jesus, through prayer and reading of His Word you gain an understanding of what your purpose is and what good works you should do. In John 15 we see how Jesus enables us to bear fruit. Not only has God chosen us, but he gives us His Holy Spirit to lead us and guide us in fulfilling our purpose and these good works that bear fruit. God loves us. He

God loves us

empowers us as long as we abide in Him. On top of that, we can ask whatever we want, as long as it is in line with His will He will grant it to us. The key is to stay close to Jesus and work on your personal relationship with him daily. He has already predestined us to bear fruit, we just have to let go of our selfishness, and follow His guidance even when we don't want to and it does not feel good. God gives us so much as His children, all we have to do is give up a little sleep, food, or time to help someone else in need. You never know what a smile or kind word does for someone. That is what He means when he says "…that your fruit should remain". When you make a difference in someone's life, it bears witness of God's love and power. It is a manifestation of the fruit of His Spirit.

Identity Principle

We are mandated to bear fruit in the kingdom of God. When we bear fruit it testifies of our connection to God.

God predestined our lives. He knows what he has for us to do. Have you factored in what God wants for you in your five year plan? Or is there only room for your will to be done. God has a plan and purpose for your life, be careful that you don't end up like the fig tree that did not bear fruit. We must do God's will so we will not be 'cut off' and unfruitful. We have to learn to hear His voice. The devil can sound just like God. So communing with Jesus and getting to know His voice like a mother knows the sound of her child in the midst of a dozen other kids is crucial. Only through time can this happen as we learn more and more about our identity in Him. To follow Jesus and take on His identity we must work at it. How hard do you work in other areas of your life?

> Beware of false prophets, who come to you in sheep's clothing, but inwardly they are ravenous wolves. You will know them by their fruits. Do men gather grapes from thorn bushes or figs from thistles? Even so, every good tree bears good fruit, but a bad tree bears bad fruit. A good tree cannot

bear bad fruit, nor can a bad tree bear good fruit. Every tree that does not bear good fruit is cut down and thrown into the fire. Therefore by their fruits you will know them. (Matthew 7:15-20 NKJV)

This fruit is displayed in our actions and draws others to us by the Spirit, attracting the unsaved and adding to the kingdom of God. So if we are bearing bad fruit, then we will know that we are not operating in the Spirit of Christ. This is also how we can know those who are unsaved, the false prophets speaking lies, and even other children of God who are operating under another spirit, being double-minded and carnal.

Identity, Purpose and the Power

A life grounded in the true identity of Jesus Christ, and striving to bear good fruit will walk on purpose. When we are on purpose and take deliberate actions every day to be holy and righteous in Christ we can begin to walk more in His power. One of the most powerful disciplines we have to change hearts, minds and the world for Christ is prayer. The Word gives us several scriptures that detail the power of asking for things in prayer in the name of Jesus.

> "And in that day you will ask Me nothing. Most assuredly, I say to you, whatever you ask the Father in My name He will give you. Until now you have asked nothing in My name. Ask, and you will receive, that your joy may be full. (John 16:23-24 NKJV)
>
> On that day you will ask in my name. I do not say to you that I will ask the Father on your behalf; (John 16:26 NRSV)
>
> And whatever you ask in My name, that I will do, that the Father may be glorified in the Son. If you ask anything in My name, I will do it. (John 14:13-14 NKJV)

These scriptures sound really nice and give us hope, but when we ask and do not receive our faith is weakened. Understanding that we must first understand where we are in the spirit, by examining ourselves in the Word of God before the Lord is the key to answered prayer.

Identity Principle

We are already right with God through the blood of Jesus, but our sins can separate us from God making Him seem far away and hard to hear.

We are already right with God through the blood of Jesus, but our sins can separate us from God making Him seem far away and hard to hear. We must be consistently repentant of our sins and communing with the Lord in prayer to understand our position in the spirit. Second, what we ask must ultimately glorify God by being in line with His character in His Word. In the gospel of John we hear the Lord Jesus explaining to His disciples the oneness of Him and God the Father. Jesus speaks of His authority to do the miraculous works that only come from God the Father, and the importance of believing in Him and His works. Just as Jesus taught His disciples, we must also be taught so that we understand. As we seek the Lord in faith for understanding we are changed, and through love desire to comply with His every will. It is in this that we are changed from glory to glory to walk closely with Jesus in the Spirit of the Lord. Once this miraculous change begins to take place in our lives we are in position to ask things in Jesus name. These things that we ask are the "greater works" that Jesus has for our lives. Webster's dictionary defines work as "labor or something made or accomplished".

If we need examples of works we should look throughout the gospels at what Jesus did for and to the people to glorify God. He healed the sick, cast out demons, made the blind to see, fed the hungry and many more works for the glory of God. In all the gospels you don't see Jesus's works as doing anything for Himself, all of His works were selfless. This should give us foundation and insight into our hearts as we ask God for things in Jesus name. What do you ask God for? Would God be glorified in what you are asking for?

Identity Principle

God's pre-defined 'good works' for each of us work together to build the kingdom of God here on earth as it is in heaven.

Just saying "in Jesus name" does not magically give you what you ask God for. Asking for something in prayer in Jesus name means that your request aligns with His character. Jesus name signifies His character, who He is. Remember from the last chapter we learned that we are to be "like Jesus", not assimilated to the world. So when we have a heart like Jesus, character like Jesus, and the mind of Christ what we request in Jesus name will be answered. We have the power to ask for anything in Jesus name as long as what we ask for is in the will of God. We also need to be walking with a pure heart towards God. So what do we do with this power? We use it to accomplish our purposes in Christ. We can rely on His power for everything we do knowing He will bring it to pass. This power is present in our weakness, God's Holy Ghost power is inside us waiting to be stirred up by calling on Jesus's name. When we as the body of Christ walk on purpose, the will of God is accomplished in our lives. Purpose defines each of us and each of our purposes work together to build the kingdom of God here on earth. God will always show Himself strong for His Namesake, His children, the body of the Lord Jesus Christ. We can always call on the name of Jesus Christ, all power is in His hands, and He will never leave us or forsake us.

Inheritance Incorruptible

> and into an inheritance that is imperishable, undefiled, and unfading, kept in heaven for you, who are being protected by the power of God through faith for a salvation ready to be revealed in the last time. In this you rejoice, even if now for a little while you have had to suffer various trials, so that the genuineness of your faith—being more precious than gold that, though perishable, is tested by fire—may be found to result in praise and glory and honor when Jesus Christ is revealed. Although you have not seen him, you love him; and even though you do not see him now, you believe in him and rejoice with an indescribable and glorious joy, for you are receiving the outcome of your faith, the salvation of your souls. (1 Peter 1:4-9 NRSV)

The apostle Peter puts some of our life trials in such eloquent terms in this scripture. God lets us know in Ecclesiastes 3:1, that there is a time and a season for everything under the sun. Now these seasons can include times of tribulation and despair in our lives, which sometimes leave us with a sense of heaviness. Sometimes this despair comes through various temptations that we succumb to in the flesh; even though we know they are out of the will of God. Other times these seasonal trials that we must endure seem endless, and feel more like a lifetime. Usually, when we look back on what happened to us, and we come out of the trial, we are able to give glory to God. This sounds unfair, but we must look at it through God's eyes and know that He trusts us in and through the situation. God knows the power He has placed in us and who He created us to be. So He feels we are able to bear the trial (1 Corinthians 10:13), and will give Him glory throughout the pain instead of wallowing in the flesh.

Identity Principle

Placing ourselves in the presence of the Lord allows us to see things clearly.

POWER and PROMISE

> What if God, desiring to show his wrath and to make known his power, has endured with much patience the objects of wrath that are made for destruction; and what if he has done so in order to make known the riches of his glory for the objects of mercy, which he has prepared beforehand for glory— (Romans 9:22-23 NRSV)

In the book of James, we learn that trials produce patience, and patience creates a perfect work in us. The trials of our faith are more precious than gold, because we are tried in the fire of the Holy Spirit in order to build our character to become more like Jesus Christ. The reward is that we are perfected from obedience to obedience, and ultimately only reach true perfection when we see Jesus face-to-face. The bible tells us that we groan internally for our heavenly bodies that will be revealed at the re-appearing of Jesus Christ; who is the One whom we love through faith, yet have never seen. We rejoice in God who loved us first, and will never leave us alone in the trails of life. He is our Comforter and very present help as we walk this life with Jesus.

Identity Principle

We must trust that God knows the power He placed in us & who He created us to be in every situation we go through in life.

Our ultimate goal should be to have life with Jesus on earth and in heaven for eternity. That is why the sufferings of this world are not comparable to the riches we will receive in glory. Whenever we have any doubts, all we have to do is look at the death Jesus went through on the cross. Our continuous sins have already been forgiven and paid for there; all we have to do is ask with a sincere heart for forgiveness. In our human nature God knows that if everything was easy we could potentially not appreciate it. If life had no

> **Our ultimate goal should be to see Jesus.**

sudden turns we might be bored. If we did not have the love of Jesus Christ we would be empty. If we did not stand for anything we would fall for everything. We have to stand for the Lover of our soul, and bear the "trials of life" for the incorruptible inheritance of eternity with our Lord and Savior Jesus Christ.

The Grey Area

There is no grey area in Jesus Christ. There is no shadow or turning in Him. Every good gift and every perfect gift is from above, and comes down from the Father of lights, with whom there is no variation or shadow of turning. (James 1:17 NKJV) Once we come to the full knowledge and power of Christ we know and understand that if we can only get before Him, we will see things clearly. The world brings darkness, disobedience brings darkness, but Christ brings light. If we waver between the two we are in the grey, but that is not Christ. When we act in this manner we are double-minded and unstable in all our ways (James 1:6-8). We must look back to Jesus and walk in His ways. Life with Jesus brings power in His name. Keeping our mind on Him brings peace and clarity to the light.

> There is no Grey Area in Jesus Christ!

As we press toward our final destination, we must do the work of God here on earth. We must actively look forward, reaching for the things that Jesus has pre-ordained and set in order for us (Philippians 3:12-14). When we move on purpose and in His power, we stay on the right path, bearing fruit. This is the example that we must set as we walk accountable to those coming behind us. It must always be clear that there is something about the name Jesus that will bring power to any dark situation. This is how we eliminate the long moment of indecision in the grey area, as we walk in our inheritance incorruptible.

POWER and PROMISE

Identity Principle

When we move on purpose and in His power we stay on the right path bearing fruit.

Wanda L. Scott

Be of good cheer
My Father says to me
I have sent my Son
so you can have peace
that in other circumstances would not be.

The world will be rough
And your problems very real
So here is a little note,
So you will know the deal.

I want you to overcome.
I want you to have life abundantly
I am going to tell you what to do,
Keep your eyes on Me.

When things get rough,
stay in my Word.
Think on things above,
and remember the wisdom you have heard.

WLS

DECLARATION: *Repeat these out loud*...and then answer the question.

1. ***I agree that Jesus is my true identity and I should strive to be like Him.*** What have you done to identify yourself with Jesus?

2. ***I agree that when I seek God for my purpose I will find power to live a fruitful life with Jesus!***
   Do you know your purpose in this season of your life?

3. ***I agree that I need to build the kingdom of God on earth with the others members of the body of Christ!***
   Can you give an example of a "good work" you have done in the name of Jesus?

Action for Abundant Life

AWARENESS: What do you ask God for? Would God be glorified in what you are asking for?

AWARENESS: How have you been aware of the world's disdain of you saying the name Jesus in your life? Are you bold enough to speak it regardless of what others think or feel?

UNDERSTANDING: Which Identity Principle in this chapter did you relate to the most? Why?

POWER and PROMISE

3
GOD'S POWER PERSONIFIED

Proverbs 24^5 - *A wise man is mightier than a strong man, and a man of **knowledge** than he who has strength. (NRSV)*

W E ARE LIVING IN DAYS WHERE MAN IS MORE intelligent and enterprising than ever before. There are a vast number of resources available to us to learn at home, on the job, or in traditional institutions. The onset of the internet has opened up an information highway to anyone who wants and is able to enter it. There is no reason for any of us to be without the power to get and obtain knowledge. That is why Dietrich Bonhoeffer, the Author of *The Cost of Discipleship* questions, "How difficult is it to draw the line with certainty between spiritual wisdom and worldly astuteness!"[1]

It seems that even though all this information is available to us, we are still in the same situation the people were in during the days of the Prophet Hosea. Then God proclaimed their fate through Hosea:

> My people are destroyed for lack of knowledge; because you have rejected knowledge, I reject you from being a priest to me. And since you have forgotten the law of your God, I also will forget your children. (Hosea 4:6)

Is this our fate today? Should we proclaim this scripture to ourselves and God's people to make sure that we don't end up "destroyed and rejected by God", failing our children. We might be in danger of perishing if we do not take seriously the *Great Commission* given by Jesus Christ to his disciples.

> Then the eleven disciples went away into Galilee, to the mountain which Jesus had appointed for them. When they saw Him, they worshiped Him; but some doubted. And Jesus came and spoke to them, saying, "All authority has been given to Me in heaven and on earth. Go therefore and make disciples of all the nations, baptizing them in the name of the Father and of the Son and of the Holy Spirit, teaching them to observe all things that I have commanded you; and lo, I am with you always, even to the end of the age." Amen. (Matthew 28:16-20 NKJV)

All the children of God are Jesus' disciples, and we must take our call seriously so we can be an effective witness for Jesus. As we grow we learn more and more about God and what the Lord's commandments are for guidance in life. This growth brings us closer to our Creator, and the Holy Spirit transforms us from moment to moment to be more like Jesus Christ. As this manifestation happens we will unconsciously show the fruit of the Spirit, and God's light of love will witness through us in our daily lives. Just being a witness as we move about our day, fulfills His commission in our little corner of the earth. This witness will help fight against the 'lack of knowledge', so our children will not be forgotten.

Identity Principle

The bible is our primary source of knowledge to the mind & character of God. We need to know it to have "life" in Jesus Christ.

The Bible

So how do we grow in this knowledge of the Lord? Many people have come before us and have died or labored in pain, so that we can have free and easy access to the bible; the Word of God. This is our primary source of knowledge to the mind and character of God. This book is living, powerful, and all-encompassing with everything we need to know to 'have life' in Jesus Christ. The bible teaches us how God has interacted with mankind and His people since the beginning of time. Unfortunately there are many who reject the Word of God, and therefore have hardened their hearts to receiving the knowledge of the Lord. The Word is truth, and is a guide to man's everyday living. It opens the door to freedom from this world, and all the things that attempt to enslave us. The Word empowers us with the guidance of the Holy Spirit to apply its meaning to our lives. In it we learn the truth and the truth sets us free from the bondage of such worldly things as addictions, hatred, violence and anything that does not display the love of God. If we do not serve God we will serve something or someone else (Romans 6:16); something that can take our attention and our mind off the one thing that offers hope and love beyond measure. We can either form our identity from this world, or from God. So in order to grow in knowledge one thing we must do is to faithfully and diligently read the Word of God, seeking the Holy Spirit's guidance in every aspect of our lives.

> The bible teaches us how God has interacted with mankind and His people since the beginning of time.

Reading the bible is a great start, but some say that "sometimes they don't understand what the bible is saying". Well, God is with us always, and knows our every want and need. In His omnipotence, He provided us with His Holy Spirit to guide us through the process of trying to get to know Him. The bible calls it "rightly dividing the Word of God". This process is how the Holy Spirit gives us insight and understanding as we seek God in reading His Word. One good practice to have is to pray to the Lord before and as you read the Word. With that prayer you have the belief that God will give you the understanding necessary to apply the Word to your life. God is a rewarder of those who diligently seek Him.

But without faith it is impossible to please him: for he that cometh to God must believe that he is, and that he is a rewarder of them that diligently seek him. (Hebrews 11:6 NRSV)

For the Lord said that those who seek Him shall find Him (Matt 7:8); so seek understanding and you will find what the Lord has for you. Foster gives us some approaches to study the bible in his book *Celebration of Discipline*. He states, "Another approach to the study of the Bible is to take a smaller book, like Ephesians or 1 John, and read it each day for the month."[2] He further admonishes us to "keep a journal of our findings."[3] It is God's desire for us to know the great mysteries of His Word (Matt 13:11); He has given us everything that we need to unlock those mysteries. "Remember the key to the Discipline of study is not reading many books, but experiencing what we do read."[4]

Identity Principle

In order to grow in knowledge we must faithfully read the Word of God, seeking the Holy Spirit's guidance.

Prayer

One might ask what else can be done to gain more knowledge of the Lord? Another key is to seek God in prayer. "He that has prayed well has studied well."[5] As you learn more about God, you will grow in awe of His power and the love that He has for us all in spite of ourselves. In this growth process we build a relationship with our Lord and savior Jesus Christ. This relationship is of a personal

> Praying directly to our heavenly Father is a gift from Jesus.

nature between us individually and the Lord. Anytime you have a personal relationship with someone you must spend time with them to nurture that relationship, and to learn more about them. The same is true with Jesus; we must get to know Him in prayer and in quiet meditation. Meditation is simply taking quiet time to think about what you have read and learned about God in His Word by His Spirit. During this meditation, God by His Holy Spirit will reveal how His Word is applicable to your life. Jesus taught His disciples how to pray in Matthew 6:9 and we must follow this model in approaching the throne of Glory.

> Our Father who art in heaven, hollowed be thy name. Thy kingdom come, thy will be done, in earth as it is in heaven. Give us this day our daily bread and forgive us our debts, as we forgive our debtors. Lead us not into temptation, but deliver us from evil. For thine is the kingdom and the power and the glory forever. AMEN. (Matthew 6:9-13)

Praying directly to our heavenly Father is a gift from Jesus, since before Jesus God's chosen people could only let their requests be known to God through the priests. Now with Jesus, the barrier has been removed and we can approach God anytime with our prayers in the name of His Son Jesus Christ. We must understand how glorious this opportunity is to talk to our Father in heaven anytime our heart desires. Our God hears our prayers whenever we need Him, and is available to answer us as we learn how to listen to Him. *Now this is the confidence that we have in Him, that if we ask anything according to His will, He hears us. And if we know that He hears us, whatever we ask, we know that we have the petitions that we have asked of Him* (1 John 5:14-15). We must utilize this powerful gift for more than our list of things we want God to do for us. Jesus teaches us that we are to pray that God's will be done on earth. That means that what God wants to happen, will happen. It is our responsibility to carry out God's will as his disciples, and the only way we can know what that is, is through His Word and praying to Him that His Spirit will reveal these things to us. "God does nothing but in answer to prayer"[6]. We must remember that when we accept Jesus Christ as our Lord and Savior, we die to the flesh and are born again to the Spirit. We stop living by and obeying what our flesh desires to do, and obediently do what God convicts, leads and empowers us to do by His Spirit. We should concentrate on the power that Jesus gives us by His Holy Spirit, so that we can do what the Lord wants. A life with Jesus provides us with authority as we get to know Him and seek Him. This authority is empowered by the Word of God and the Holy Spirit so God's will is done through us.

Identity Principle

We are to pray that God's will be done on earth. It is our responsibility to carry out God's will on earth as His Spirit reveals it to us.

We are also encouraged to pray for one another. When we do this we edify and build up the body of Christ, for as we pray for others we are blessed ourselves. Remember that although we are individuals all trying to serve the Lord, spiritually we are one body through Christ Jesus. We as individuals are members of the family of God. The family of God works together as "members" that bond together in unity and serve one common purpose – the work of God through Jesus Christ our Savior. As we build up the body of Christ through prayer, we are building up ourselves spiritually. "To pray is to change. Prayer is the central avenue God uses to transform us"[7]. Prayer changes things. One awesome example in the bible of the power of prayer is when Paul and Silas were in jail praying all night, and the Lord supernaturally set them free.

> About midnight Paul and Silas were praying and singing hymns to God, and the prisoners were listening to them. Suddenly there was an earthquake, so violent that the foundations of the prison were shaken; and immediately all the doors were opened and everyone's chains were unfastened. When the jailer woke up and saw the prison doors wide open, he drew his sword and was about to kill himself, since he supposed that the prisoners had escaped.

> But Paul shouted in a loud voice, "Do not harm yourself, for we are all here." The jailer called for lights, and rushing in, he fell down trembling before Paul and Silas. Then he brought them outside and said, "Sirs, what must I do to be saved?" They answered, "Believe on the Lord Jesus, and you will be saved, you and your household." (Acts 16:25-31 NRSV)

When we seek the Lord with our cares, concerns, and requests, He feels honored and is inclined to help us. *Therefore I say unto you, What things soever you desire, when ye pray, believe that ye receive them, and ye shall have them* (Mark 11:24). God says that we should not be anxious about anything, but bring all our requests and things we are worried about to him in prayer (Philippians 4:6). Not only can we change things for ourselves, but we act as interceders for others and stand in the gap for them when they can't or will not go to the Lord for help. God desires that some of His children give themselves continually to Him in prayer, and to the ministry of His Word (Acts 6:4). Prayer is a ministry itself, as it speaks directly to the Lord of our individual and corporate needs. There are people who are "called" or "compelled" to pray for others all the time. Prayer is a direct communication path to God through Jesus', and allows conversation with the Lord as we speak with Him about the knowledge we gain about Him.

> God always knows the best answer to any problem.

> But I say unto you, Love your enemies, bless them that curse you, do good to them that hate you, and pray for them which despitefully use you, and persecute you (Matthew 5:44).

Not only are we to pray for ourselves and other family members and friends, but we must pray for our enemies also. This is done with God's love for them, and the understanding that God is the only one who can help them defeat the evil attitudes and character that they are displaying. This behavior clouds their hearts. Prayer to God helps Him help us, by changing the circumstances we find ourselves in with them. We are taught in the Word to love above all. This is the greatest commandment because God is love, but it is also the hardest one to accomplish in our flesh. That is why we must walk in the Spirit and in the character of God to accomplish His will. If we really think about it, praying for our enemies is the best thing we could do, because it releases our hurt, anger, and allows us to forgive. Even though that is not our first inclination, we should always go to the God for guidance and strength. God always knows the best answer to any problem. If we do not forgive others, God is not free to forgive us (Mark 11:25). Prayer is healing; it is a release to the only person who has the power to change situations in our lives. Prayer brings us more in tune with the character of God as we get to know him better.

Identity Principle

Praying for our enemies is the best thing we could do because it releases our hurt, anger, and allows us to forgive.

The Role of the Local Church

The Lord knows His children. He knows that we are not always as obedient as we should be in reading His Word. Therefore He has provided us with preachers and teachers who can help us grow with messages and application from His Word.

> And I will give you shepherds according to My heart, who will feed you with knowledge and understanding. (Jeremiah 3:15 NKJV)

The local church is His house of prayer (Mark 11:17), built to provide a place for believers to gather together in fellowship and praise. "When the people of God meet together, there often comes a sense of being "gathered" into one mind, becoming of one accord (Phil. 3:15)."[8] The church is another source for us to gain knowledge about God. As we praise God and hear the preached Word from God, we are in the presence of the Holy Spirit which ministers through the preached Word to our needs. For the Lord said whenever two are three are gathered together in His name, He will be there also (Matthew 18:20). "When we are truly gathered into worship, things occur that could never occur alone."[9] The local church usually offers preaching and teaching several days of the week. We are encouraged in the Word of God not to forsake the assembling of ourselves together (Hebrews 10:25). Assembling together as the children of God should take on many different forms, such as your family unit, home fellowships, small groups at various locations, or just time with one other believer speaking of the goodness of God in our lives. Local churches can be the primary source of knowledge gathering that some children of God use, but really does not provide for the personal relationship that is needed or desired by God. God desires our one-on-one attention the most.

> The fear of the LORD is the beginning of knowledge; fools despise wisdom and instruction (Proverbs 1:7 NRSV).

The word fear in Hebrew means reverence, and is applicable in this passage in the book of Proverbs. As we grow to know God we reverence Him in His awesome power and love. This reverence is a driving factor for us to want to get to know Him more. There are people out there who do not want to acknowledge that there is a higher power than them. They also do not want to accept that God is the Creator and Ruler of all things; therefore they come up with foolishness such as the Theory of Evolution to try and justify their unbelief. These people have hardened hearts, and are not open to receive the one true God. They usually believe that they are already knowledgeable enough, and do not need to be taught anything about God, and therefore lack godly wisdom needed to understand true life. We must revere the Lord, and always be open to learn and be taught more about Him. His ways are higher than our ways and His thoughts are higher than our thoughts (Isaiah 55:9). We will never completely understand all we need to know about our Lord until we meet Him face to face. We must maintain a teachable spirit, and an open heart to godly instruction.

The Grey Area

As we learn how to grow in knowledge we are able to pass this information on to our children and others. This knowledge will help them as they enter the grey areas of their lives. We are not just responsible for ourselves in gaining knowledge, but we must also pass that knowledge on to our families and others that we love. Truthfully that would include everyone that we come in contact with, as we are to love others as we love ourselves. In this love we feel for God and thus for others, we are inclined to share the truths that we are learning. This knowledge is powerful and can make the difference in our choices as we move down life's path. Truth will always triumph over a lie, as long as we believe it by faith. Believing truth empowers us and sets us free. This freedom manifests in our lives as power and authority which can be seen by others as we walk with the Lord. This belief impels us to testify of the "good news" (Gospel) of Jesus Christ, the more we learn of His righteousness.

Identity Principle

It is not good enough to just speak, teach, and share God's Word, we have to live it.

In sharing this knowledge, we have to teach others how to get this knowledge on their own. We are not just giving them godly wisdom, but showing them the vehicles to gain more knowledge on their own. This will provide them with resources to make right decisions when faced with the choices the world will throw at them. We have to make sure that they will not just depend on us, but on God for guidance in His Word. The only dependence that is ever needed is on God, and we have to be careful to convey that in sharing the knowledge of God.

It is not good enough to just speak, teach, and share God's Word, we have to live it. We have to walk in the knowledge of Jesus Christ. We have to acknowledge Him in everything we do. Our children and others have to see us committed to gaining knowledge through our actions. This action should be consistent in our reading of the bible, praying, and fellowshipping with other children of God, and serving God through helping and caring for others. They must also see the supernatural power of God working in and amongst the children of God. Our authority in Christ Jesus should be modeled in everyday life, as well as in signs, miracles and wonders. These actions have to be taught to our children so they will know the right things to do and expect from a life with Jesus. The Word of God says that "he shall die from lack of instruction. And in the greatness of his folly he shall go astray" (Proverbs 5:23 NKJV). We are responsible for teaching our children because the Word says that we should train up a child in the way that he should go, and he will not depart from it when he is old. This level of reverence and accountability will make impressions on others as they grow in the knowledge of God.

> We should acknowledge God in everything we do!

And when Simon saw that through the laying on of the apostles' hands the Holy Spirit was given, he offered them money, saying, "Give me this power also, that anyone whom I lay hands on may receive the Holy Spirit." But Peter said to him, "Your money perish with you, because you thought that the gift of God could be purchased with money! (Acts 8:8-20 NKJV)

This authority and power will compel others to seek God for that kind of relationship with Him. Our actions speak louder than our words. The prophet Habakkuk proclaims the truth, *"For the earth will be filled with the knowledge of the glory of the LORD, as the waters cover the sea."* (Habakkuk 2:14).

Wanda L. Scott

Day to Day
What Words do you say?
Day to Day
What do your actions display -
about you?

In the bible Jesus led the way.
In the bible Jesus did just as He said.
In the bible the people were healed and fed.
In the bible – Day to Day
Jesus showed us the way.

Did you know that God has a way for you to go?
Did you know that Jesus will help you grow?
Did you know the Holy Spirit guides you the more you know?

Day to Day
Whose Words do you say?
Words of Healing and Love
that show kindness God's way.

Day to Day
Whose actions do you display?
Power and Authority
with Jesus leading the way.

WLS

DECLARATION: *Repeat these out loud*...and then answer the question.

1. ***I agree that in order to grow in knowledge I must faithfully read the Word of God, seeking the Holy Spirit's guidance.***
   Will you challenge yourself to set a disciplined study schedule?

2. ***I agree that praying for my enemies is the best thing I can do because it releases my hurt, anger and allows me to forgive.***
   Name one of your enemies you need to pray for.

3. ***I agree that it is not good enough to just speak, teach and share God's word, I must live it!***
   Give at least one example of living God's word.

Action for Abundant Life

AWARENESS: Do you believe that you have power and authority in Christ Jesus? If not examine your faith in the truth of the Word of God.

AWARENESS: Have you been as dedicated as you should be to study and rightly dividing the Word of God as His disciple? Why or Why not?

UNDERSTANDING: Which Identity Principle in this chapter did you relate to the most? Why?

POWER and PROMISE

4
HOW TO DEFINE SUCCESS

Joshua 1 [7] Only be strong and very courageous, being careful to act in accordance with all the law that my servant Moses commanded you; do not turn from it to the right hand or to the left, so that you may be successful wherever you go. [8] This book of the law shall not depart out of your mouth; you shall meditate on it day and night, so that you may be careful to act in accordance with all that is written in it. For then you shall make your way prosperous, and then you shall be successful.

OK YOU ARE SAYING TO YOURSELF, I know my true identity as a child of God, and I am gaining knowledge in the Word, so now where do I go from here? The Lord says that if we meditate on His Word we shall prosper and have good success. So whatever we do and wherever we go, if we stay true to His Word and the guidance of His Holy Spirit, we will not ultimately fail. God has a purpose and a plan for all of our lives. *For we are His workmanship, created in Christ Jesus for good works, which God prepared beforehand that we should walk in them (Ephesians 2:10).* It is up to us to seek God and find out what our purpose is in conjunction with His plan. It is up to us to decide to follow God's plan. It is a choice. We have to purposely live according to God's instructions for our lives. When we know that purpose, and follow God's plan not ours, we will find success, godly success.

Everything is a choice.

If we are truly finding our identity in the Lord, then we look to Him for who He has called us to be, and what He planned for us to do. The bible says to commit your work to the LORD, and your plans will be established (Proverbs 16:3). This promise also shows that when we are committed to following the will of

Identity Principle

It is up to us to seek God to find out what our purpose is in conjunction with His plan, & then follow it.

God, then whatever it is that we do in His will, will be established or happen. A passage of scripture in the book of Proverbs explains that many are the plans in a man's heart, but it is the Lord that directs his steps. So we might have one idea in our minds of what good success should be, but if this idea does not line up with the character and will of God, then we are not guaranteed good success. All of us have had a good idea before. We might have even worked hard to make that good idea a reality. If that good idea was our own, and we did not consult God about it, then its success could be short lived. It might not bring about the kind of godly prosperity that could have been achieved if we had looked to God for guidance and direction. We can accomplish some things without God, but not the things that will last when we are gone, and that matter to God. How do you want others to remember you? What legacy do you want to leave behind? Paul makes it clear in his letter to the Church of Corinth the difference between what we can do and what we should do; because the things we should do will come easy and will not require us to compromise our commitment to God.

> All things are lawful for me," but not all things are helpful. "All things are lawful for me," but I will not be enslaved by anything (1 Corinthians 6:12 NRSV).

We can do anything we want, but is what we want good for us according to God? Good is not always God. If we do what we want we might get caught up in something that we cannot get out of? "God does not only want you to be successful in theory; He has given you all you need to be successful in reality."[1]

Profiting for Our Good

> Thus says the LORD, your Redeemer, the Holy One of Israel: "I am the LORD your God, who teaches you to profit, who leads you in the way you should go. O that you had hearkened to my commandments! Then your peace would have been like a river, and your righteousness like the waves of the sea (Isaiah 48:17 18)

Who is the Lord of your life? Is it your fleshy desires? Is it your 'man' or 'woman'? What or who do you look to for guidance? The only right answer is God. When we finally realize this, sometimes we have already gone down our own destructive path. God knows how hard it is sometimes to not do what we want first. He is a gracious and forgiving God if we seek Him and ask for forgiveness and help. As children of God we must break down our own will and surrender to God's will. When we do, the benefits are amazing. Did you know that every good and every perfect gift comes from God? (James 1:17) God wants to give you a good gift, the gift of good success.

When we as God's children do seek Him, He teaches us to profit (v17d). The bible says money answers all things, but we must not love it more than God because it is not always *the* answer. It is God's will for us to profit, but that does not have to mean just monetarily. We can profit spiritually, mentally, and in health also. When we let the Lord teach us by His Holy Spirit, we are lead down the right path and doors can seem to just open up for us. We as God's children do and will profit by His guidance. In His Word He says that He will go before us and make the crooked places straight (Isaiah 45:2).

Identity Principle

It is God's will for us to profit spiritually, mentally, and in health.

God always gives us more than we can imagine if we are walking in obedience to Him. As we live a life in accordance with what is right, God will give us peace like a river. The bumps in life will not stop us for long; we will flow right over them like the water does over the rocks of the river. In its natural state, have you ever seen anything block the flow of a river? That can be God's peace in our lives. Isaiah proclaims that God will also give us righteousness like the waves of the sea. As we live for God we walk in righteousness through Jesus Christ. Righteousness is doing what is *right* in God's sight. If we think about the waves of the sea and how they can powerfully move ships and other objects, we can compare that to the righteousness of God through Christ Jesus. With the Lord's righteousness we can move mountains.

> And when the disciples saw it, they marveled, saying, "How did the fig tree wither away so soon?" So Jesus answered and said to them, "Assuredly, I say to you, if you have faith and do not doubt, you will not only do what was done to the fig tree, but also if you say to this mountain, 'Be removed and be cast into the sea,' it will be done. And whatever things you ask in prayer, believing, you will receive." (Matthew 21:20-22)

Mountains can be any obstacle or challenge that is deterring your success. God wants us to prosper and have good success. He has laid it all out for us in His Word for our good.

> "And now, Israel, what does the LORD your God require of you, but to fear the LORD your God, to walk in all his ways, to love him, to serve the LORD your God with all your heart and with all your soul, and to keep the commandments and statutes of the LORD, which I command you this day for your good? (Deuteronomy 10:12-13)

There are a lot of things that we are told to do for our good. We are told to go to the dentist every six months to have our teeth checked and cleaned for the good of our teeth. For the good of the country we are commanded to pay taxes. For the good of community, most of us pay some sort of homeowner's fee.

Most of these we do as part of a regular routine without too much thought or opposition. Most of these we do not question, even though they are not usually anything we would say we want to do. But it seems when it comes to our commitment and duty unto God, we have plenty of questions, shortcuts and push-backs. Why do we as children of God resist doing the things that are for the greatest good? The list outlined in Deuteronomy 10 does not seem too hard until we get to the part about God's commandments. Do you know what God commands for your life? If you learn about and follow Jesus Christ you will. It is easier to live as a servant to Jesus Christ than the command to give what feels like almost half of our paychecks to the government in taxes.

The bible says that we must fear the Lord God. Remember, in this sense fear is defined as reverence for the Lord. We must acknowledge and give proper respect to God for his love and power. If we just look at our lives and this world around us we can see how awesome He is as our Creator. This knowledge should give us incentive to live by His Word, loving and serving Him with all our heart and soul. Now this can be hard on our own. If we are a child of God, we are not left alone to accomplish this in our own power. We have the Holy Spirit to lead and guide us as we grow and mature in God. Just as we are only expected to pay taxes according to our income level, we are only expected to walk in the ways of God we know about, and are empowered to walk in. As babes in Christ we are not held accountable for what we don't know, because we have not had time to grow in knowledge. But we must also remember that the Bible does say to him or her who knows to do good and does not do it, it is sin (James 4:17). God knows the truth in your heart, so our lip-service saying we did not know is not valid to our Omniscient (all-knowing) God. As we grow in our knowledge of the Lord, we love Him more and more, and can't help but to serve Him with all our heart and soul. That is just what love does, it gives. Once you accept Jesus into your heart

> That is what Love does…it gives.

not just as your Savior, but also as your Lord, your heart is opened to love in ways you never knew were possible.
We are to keep God's commandments by following Jesus. We take these and apply them to our present day lives as a litmus test of where the Holy Spirit needs to start doing a work of love in our lives. By giving our lives to Christ we are not under the law, but saved by grace. The law condemns and brings us to the awareness of rights and wrongs, but grace forgives and does a work of love in our hearts so that we begin to live according to the character of Jesus Christ. The sacrifice of Jesus Christ empowers us to exemplify all that the law could not accomplish. The expression of love that God displayed for us by sacrificing His Son Jesus, gives to us the power to do good works through Christ Jesus. We accomplish these good works by the power of the Holy Spirit and the knowledge of the Word of God. God knew without the love of God in our hearts we would never be all that He has called us to be. That is why it is for our good to do all of these things He has laid out for us, so we can stay in line with His will and walk out our predestined works. Since we are created by God, He is the authority on what is best for us. So let's be just as obedient to His will for us as we are to the things the world commands us to do. The things that He commands are for a greater eternal good.

Good Success –vs- Bad Success

This *good success* given by God must mean that there can be *bad success.* The phrase "bad success" seems like an oxymoron. So let us first try and understand that if God declares that we will have good success, than it is success that comes through living by His Word. So this good success is actually godly success. Godly success is any accomplishment that is achieved in the will of God; for we can only be in God's will if we are walking in God's Spirit. "If you have the Lord Jesus Christ as your Savior and the power of the Holy Spirit resident in you, you can do all things that the Lord leads you to do. To underestimate yourself or sell yourself short is to underestimate God in you and to sell His abilities short."[2] Since we have defined good success, then it is easy to define bad success. Bad success is any accomplishment that is achieved outside the will of God. This success can be laborious and does not fulfill in us the peace and prosperity that only God's success can provide. When we are on this path to success we could run into all types of roadblocks and setbacks, and might often toil greatly in the process. In good success the Lord's promises all fall into place and doors can be supernaturally opened for us.

Identity Principle

Every child of God has purpose in life that will lead to the 'good success' the Lord desires for us.

Good success also ties directly in with us as children of God walking on purpose. The Word of God says that all things work together for the good of those who love the Lord and are called according to His purpose (Romans 8:28). Every child of God has purpose and within this purposeful life is where each of us will find the godly 'good success' the Lord desires for us. Have you sought the Lord for your purpose? God is a rewarder of those who diligently seek Him, and He will reward you with revealing your purpose so you can have good success. This purpose is carried out in the manifestation of your individual God given gifts. You were born with talents, skills and abilities to enable you to carry out your purpose. These along you're your Spiritual gifts must be developed in the anointing and guidance of the Holy Spirit. This development comes by yielding to God, practicing, applying, and exercising them to the glory of God.[3]

> Good Success is actually Godly Success

There are many people in this world who have achieved bad success. They come to a place where they have all the money, power, and fame that the world can provide, but they can still be empty inside. Bad success usually lives up to worldly standards and expectations. Looking from the world's point of view things can appears to be all one could ever want our dream of. The world looks on the outside, God looks at the inside (1 Samuel 16:7). The world identifies with the nice clothes, fancy cars, and the luxurious homes of these successful people. Their monetary status tells the world that they can have and do anything that they want. God's love, purpose and good success provide you with peace in Jesus Christ. This peace will sustain you when all that the world identifies as success fails you. Jesus' peace is a peace that surpasses all human understanding (Philippians 4:6-8).

The World's Success

The world constantly broadcasts their definition of success on our TV screens. We see images in magazines of the world's idea of success. In our streets our young people are influenced by what they see other people wear and drive as a testimony of their success, even if they are selling drugs or stealing to get it. Our children idolize singers, rappers, and athletes who the world says are successful. They identify with their success stories as fed to them by the media. They identify with what their friends say is cool, looking to be popular or successful by having the right friends or material possessions. Our young people believe that these people that they see and want to be like are successful. They are lured into identifying with the world and bad success.

Our young people are not the only ones who are influenced by the images of success we see in the world. If we truthfully allow ourselves to reflect on our actions and behaviors at different times in our lives, we will see the worlds influence on us, in its definition of success. We live in the world, but have to stay in the Word of God to feed our mind and spirit. God's Word is

> The knowledge of God reminds us of what is really important.

cleansing to our mind and spirit. It renews our strength and our commitment to the Lord when our spirit is weary form the pressures of the world. Knowledge of the right way and the truth of God's Word are the only defenses against worldly influences. This knowledge of God reminds us of what is really important, and that material things can never be a substitute for the love of our Lord. We are reminded of our responsibility in Paul's letter to the Romans, *Do not be conformed to this world but be transformed by the renewal of your mind, that you may prove what is the will of God, what is good and acceptable and perfect.* (Romans 12:2 NRSV)

Identity Principle

The knowledge of God's Word reminds us that material things can never be a substitute for Him.

Living Examples

We have to be a living example of godly success for our children to combat the world's examples of bad success. If our children and others only see the examples of bad success, and only hear us talk about good success, then their perspective will be skewed. This perspective could lead them to believe that bad success is truly the way or at least worth a try if they are not strong enough in faith. We have to have our own success stories to tell of how godly living made doors open for us and caused us to prosper. When material things are gained in good success and kept in the proper perspective, not idolized, there is nothing wrong with having them. We have to be clear in our living that we can have a nice car, house, and plenty of clothes to choose from, and that there is nothing wrong with that when the Lord has been your source and you acknowledge Him for it. Our example of giving to those in need and serving others has to be prevalent to balance out and show the heart of God's provision for our lives.

> Teach those who are rich in this world not to be proud and not to trust in their money, which is so unreliable. Their trust should be in God, who richly gives us all we need for our enjoyment. Tell them to use their money to do good. They should be rich in good works and generous to those in need, always being ready to share with others. By doing this they will be storing up their treasure as a good foundation for the future so that they may experience true life (1 Timothy 6:17-19 NLT).

As the body of Christ we should have as many good success stories to fill our news broadcasts, papers and radio waves with as the world does. These stories should be just as prominent as the latest entertainment news. Our children should not just see us living our lives holy and righteous following God's Word to good success, but our friends and neighbors also. We must surround ourselves with God's people - other members in Christ - to keep ourselves grounded and accountable. Examples of being led by the Holy Spirit and the fulfillment of God's promises should be seen every day. These people and their stories are out there, and they are living victoriously through the power of the Holy Spirit. We have to promote ourselves in our lives and the lives of those around us, just as much or more than the world. We have to fill the earth with the story of God's glory. We have to build each other up while building ourselves up. It is written that they will know that we are His disciples by the love we have for one another (John 13:35).

Identity Principle

When material things are gained in good success and not idolized, there is nothing wrong with having them when the Lord has been your source.

The Grey Area

In renewing our minds we enable ourselves to be accountable to the younger generation and our children. We have to make sure that they are armored with the Word of God also, so when they are bombarded with these images of bad success they can keep them in the proper perspective. This assures them of their guaranteed success in the Lord. They need to know that the Lord has good success for them as they grow in getting to know God in the Word, and walk in the will of God on purpose. These truths will free them from the enslavement that the world will bring on them to just obtain material gain. If they are not grounded in the love of God that is manifested through us as the body of Christ, then they will look for that love in material things. If we don't teach them by example how to walk in the will of God and achieve success, then they will be inclined to believe otherwise. This is part of the grey area that they will encounter, and will be allowed to make a choice of which way to precede. This choice in the grey area is directly tied to our ability to give the same level of consistent messages that the world is giving them

> There is guaranteed success in the Lord.

Success God's way
can I achieve it?
The challenges I face
cause me not to believe it.

But if I stay focused on
God's predestined way,
His Spirit will lead me
and guide me to a more perfect way.

Godly success is more than possible
it is promised in His Word.
The Lord wants us to be successful,
so His voice through us can be heard.

WLS

DECLARATION: *Repeat these out loud...and then answer the question.*

1. ***I agree that it is up to me to seek God for my purpose in conjunction with His plan, and then to follow it.***
   Are you following God's plan or yours?

2. ***I agree that it is God's will for me to profit spiritually, mentally and in good health.***
   Have you profited in your life with Jesus?

3. ***I agree that the Lord desires for me to have good success.***
   Have you mistaken bad success for good success?

Action for Abundant Life

AWARENESS: Do you believe that "good success" is ONLY achieved in the will of God? How does that change your perspective on your past achievements?

AWARENESS: Can you give at least one example of "good success" in your life with Jesus?

UNDERSTANDING: Which Identity Principle in this chapter did you relate to the most? Why?

5
GROWING BEYOND PLAYING CHURCH

Ephesians 4 *[15] Instead, we will speak the truth in love, growing in every way more and more like Christ, who is the head of his body, the church. [16] He makes the whole body fit together perfectly. As each part does its own special work, it helps the other parts grow, so that the whole body is healthy and growing and full of love. (NLT)*

YOU ARE THE REAL CHURCH, and the Spirit of Jesus Christ is in you. Wherever you go the church of Jesus Christ is represented. Does your time together in your local church fellowship look like the verses above? Is every member working together in unity doing their share? Does everyone help to accomplish growth in the knowledge of God through loving one another? If not, you might be "playing church". We have established in previous chapters what the real church or the body of Christ is. Now we look at what we have allowed the world to turn some of our local church fellowship times into.

Identity Principle

You are the real church, and the Spirit of Jesus Christ is in you. Wherever you go the church of Jesus Christ is represented.

As we move in so many different directions satisfying the flesh every day of the week, and sometimes on Sunday, the question is asked, "How is it possible to live the life of faith when we grow weary of prayer, when we lose our taste for reading the Bible, and when sleep, food, and sensuality deprive us of the joy of communion with God?"[1] The question itself lends to the answer, the satisfying of the flesh has deprived us of communion with the Spirit of God. This gradual or not so gradual lean toward the easy, inherit nature of the flesh has infiltrated the body of Christ one member at a time. We have allowed it to overpower our determination to adhere to the will of the Spirit of God.

We as the church are called to be different. We are called 'peculiar people' in the Word of God. We are called to be sanctified or 'set apart'. If we know what the Word says, how did we get confused into thinking that what the world does is ok for us to do as the body? That is the problem; we don't know the Word and don't take the one-on-one time to personally get to know God like we should. We are so dependent on others to tell us what the bible says, we don't read it for ourselves. When we do this we leave the character, love and teachings of God up to the interpretation of man, not questioning and allowing the Holy Spirit to bring us to all understanding. We have become lazy as children of God. The Word itself speaks on laziness in Proverbs (15:19), and how its end is destitution. We must know the Word for ourselves in order for the church to function as one organism in Spirit and in truth. If God's teachings in His Word are not in us, then we will act any kind of way according to the flesh, which is the world's way.

Identity Principle

To break the cycle of worldliness in the universal church, the individuals in the body of Christ have to stop 'playing' in our walk with Christ.

To break the cycle of worldliness in the universal church, we have to start with the individuals in the body of Christ. That means you and I, the members that have started to act in dysfunction. If the corporate church is "playing", that means that we are "playing" when it comes to our individual walk with God. Is it possible that you are praising God in words, but your heart is far from Him? Have some of us as the children of God lost communication in our personal relationship with Jesus. We have if we are not looking to or hearing from the Lord in our decisions and in our actions. We must start with ourselves because we are supposed to be changing from glory to glory as we are transformed into the image of Christ.

> But we all, with unveiled face, beholding as in a mirror the glory of the Lord, are being transformed into the same image from glory to glory, just as by the Spirit of the Lord. (2 Corinthians 3:18 NKJV)

How can we change if the transforming power of Christ is absent from our lives because we have ceased to hear from God? Our personal relationship provides the power to transform us to be like Christ Jesus. When we prioritize this relationship we will begin to hear God as He desires.

Once Foolish

> For we ourselves were once foolish, disobedient, led astray, slaves to various passions and pleasures, passing our days in malice and envy, hated by men and hating one another; but when the goodness and loving kindness of God our Savior appeared, he saved us, not because of deeds done by us in righteousness, but in virtue of his own mercy, by the washing of regeneration and renewal in the Holy Spirit, which he poured out upon us richly through Jesus Christ our Savior, so that we might be justified by his grace and become heirs in hope of eternal life. (Titus 3:3-7 NRSV)

Can you easily testify to this passage of scripture? In this letter to Titus, Paul is encouraging Him to empathize with the new believers in Crete and lead them in perfecting their walk. This empathy is based on the premise that at one point or another we have all been 'foolish' at the very least. If you are human you have been at least one of the descriptive words used in the passage of scripture in Titus. This behavior probably led you down a path that was not of God, causing you to walk in the flesh.

In God's Word we frequently see Him divinely using the conjunction starting verse 4, BUT, that always leads us to the positive side with Jesus Christ. Even though we were once foolish, God introduced us to the goodness and loving kindness of Jesus who saved us and justified us by His grace in hope of eternal life with Him. This revelation that allows us to open up our heart to the knowledge of Jesus Christ (1 Corinth. 4:6) is the precursor to the entrance of our helper, the Holy Spirit. With the help of the Holy Spirit ushering us through our growth process in God, we can deny the disobedience, malice, and hatred we are prone to in the flesh. We must always look for that divine empowerment in the Word that shows us the right way, the light on the other side of the tunnel.

At times we can dress up the gift of salvation and not talk about the cost of salvation, since the initial entrance seems easy. The Lord knows his children and He knew we must come in as babies and be fed milk, and then as we grew we could start to really digest the 'meat' of the Word. Have you taken the gift of salvation and stayed on milk (baby food), which is for new believers for far too long? We have to understand that we need to grow and learn the cost of salvation, which is discipleship unto Jesus Christ. We must all come to a greater revelation of Jesus. He is not pleased when we don't grow in our understanding and in His power. The key is to always walk as children of God striving to grow the kingdom of God. We all must teach and share with others what we have learned so they will not make the same mistakes staying immature in God too long. The Lord is faithful to forgive us if we ask for forgiveness. We cannot take His grace and mercy for granted, because for the one that knows to do good and does not, it is sin. The kingdom of God's growth and proliferation depends on all of us

> Wake up! Strengthen what little remains, for even what is left is almost dead. I find that your actions do not meet the requirements of my God. Go back to what you heard and believed at first; hold to it firmly. Repent and turn to me again. If you don't wake up, I will come to you suddenly, as unexpected as a thief. "Yet there are some in the church in Sardis who have not soiled their clothes with evil. They will walk with me in white, for they are worthy. All who are victorious will be clothed in white. I will never erase their names from the Book of Life, but I will announce before my Father and his angels that they are mine. (Revelations 3:2-5 NLT)

As children of God we must understand that we are saved by no works of our own, but as a gift of mercy and grace and the washing of regeneration. Regeneration in this situation is to be "re-gened". When we were born in the flesh we had the genes of our parents and were prone to all of their physical, medical, and social baggage. When we are born again in the Spirit we are re-gened into the family of Jesus Christ. We became heir to the promises of God, kings and queens, a royal priesthood, and wonderfully and fearfully made! With Jesus Christ our genes are from the Lord God. Our heredity is changed. According to the Common English Dictionary, heredity is defined as the 'transmission from one generation to another of genetic factors that determine individual characteristics: responsible for the resemblances between parents and offspring'. We take on God's characteristics and resemble Him! We are regened with His power and authority by the Holy Spirit. In this our very life is made new, and we are changed to

Identity Principle

When we are born again in the Spirit we are regened into the family of Jesus Christ. We became heir to the promise inheriting the heredity of Christ!

live a supernatural life with Jesus. As we grow up from this new birth by the Spirit of God we obtain our inheritance by faith. Our salvation is poured out richly on us, and all we have to do is walk in it to become all He has called us to be. We are commanded to grow in God, walk in the Spirit, and always be mindful that we were once foolish. When we seek the guidance of the Holy Spirit, we are guided on how we can reach others who are still foolish with our testimony of God's saving grace and the washing of His regeneration, making all things new.

Growing Up

> But to each one of us grace was given according to the measure of Christ's gift. And He Himself gave some to be apostles, some prophets, some evangelists, and some pastors and teachers, for the equipping of the saints for the work of ministry, for the edifying of the body of Christ, till we all come to the unity of the faith and of the knowledge of the Son of God, to a perfect man, to the measure of the stature of the fullness of Christ; that we should no longer be children, tossed to and fro and carried about with every wind of doctrine, by the trickery of men, in the cunning craftiness of deceitful plotting (Ephesians 4:7, 11-14 NKJV)

God gave each of us gifts to minister to each other with as the body of Christ. We are to take the gifts that God gave us and use them for "the equipping of the saints for the work of ministry", and "for the edifying of the body of Christ". If we have not moved out of the dysfunction and are still being foolish in our actions, these gifts will be misused, because we are not in the Spirit receiving proper guidance for the administration (use) of the gifts. This is crucial in the passing on of the faith and the ability for the church universal to be the one that Jesus is coming back for. Although in this passage of scripture we mainly see leadership gifts, there are many more that are necessary to do the work needed in the kingdom of God (1

Corinthians 12, Ephesians 4, Romans 12). Just as we the body of Christ all have to work together, the successful use of the gifts God gives us is equally important in us individually. The Word of God says the gifts and calling of God are irrevocable (Romans 11:29). Even if we are not operating in the Spirit, but in the flesh we can still use the gifts God gave us in disobedience. Many are utilizing the gifts of God, but not as the Lord has ordained them. We have to recognize what is from the Lord, and use it to glorify Him. We have to teach each other and new believers how to live for God and what is pleasing in His sight. This will help them make better choices individually, so that corporately our gifts can work together for the good to glorify God in our fellowships. As we teach, we as the body will be less susceptible to the lies the enemy plants, and his constant attempts to creep worldliness into the life and activity of the body of Christ.

> We have to move away from just being believing that Sunday morning is the only day to worship and that that is what God desires.

Identity Principle

The primary way to teach and disciple is through the witness of a life exemplified by love, obedience and the fruit of God's Spirit.

We know if the corporate church is in dysfunction, then that means that we as the body are not functioning in unity by the Holy Spirit. We have to get back to the fundamentals of ministry, teaching and discipling as Christ did here on earth. The primary way to teach and disciple is through the witness of a life exemplified by love, obedience and the fruit of God's Spirit. Jesus discipled the twelve and the others who followed Him by living a life submitted and obedient to God before them, coupled it with teaching and the demonstration of supernatural power in the earth. The proclaimed Word will never lose its place in the life of the body of Christ (the church), but we have to move away from just being believing that Sunday morning is the only day to worship and that that is what God desires. We have to walk with the Lord and talk with the Lord every day. In the Psalms one and in the book of Joshua we are told that we have to meditate on the Word day and night. This sounds like a tall order, but it is not unfamiliar as this is what the prescription has been throughout the bible. Dysfunction is proliferated in the universal church by the disparity in bible readers amongst the body of Christ. Jesus' death on the cross was in the human sense a horrible sacrifice that we might have the gift of salvation; but spiritually it was a victory. So as Christ endured the cross, we must endure the whining of the flesh as we subject it to the Spirit of God on a daily basis so we can have the victory. We must combat the desire to sleep, eat, and watch television or anything else that rises up to distract us from the knowledge of God in our one-on-one personal time with Him. We must fight to walk victoriously as children of God, and take the worldliness out of our life with Jesus.

Teach and Disciple

The prophet Hosea proclaimed in the Old Testament scripture that our people are destroyed by lack of knowledge. Who taught you what you know about the Lord? Did you have a model of a godly man or woman in your life? How have you formulated in your mind what a child of God should look like? These are the fundamental questions facing the children of God today of all ages.

> We must show them the difference between life and life more abundantly.

With children having children at such an early age, there is no such thing as "Grandma who used to take me to church or read the bible to me". We are living in a different age where all children do not know that "*Yes, Jesus loves me*". We have to approach the necessity of passing along the faith from a different perspective, but with the same passion. We have to teach our children in a way that they can hear, learn and become excited about what Christ did for them on Calvary. We have to teach those who have come to Christ in a different season of their lives, with application so that they can start to renew their minds in the transforming Word of God. Whether these babies in Christ are children or seasoned in the ways of the world, we have to meet them where they are and minister to them the love and the ways of Christ. This way they will have a chance to become one of the body that operates in the unity of one Spirit, and can see the kingdom of God on earth as it is in heaven.

Identity Principle

We have to teach those who are seasoned in the ways of the world with application so that they can start to renew their minds in the transforming Word of God.

Now as we teach them, we also have to disciple them. Discipleship is to teach by being a walking example of how to apply what is taught to everyday life. Accepting Christ is easy, salvation is a free gift, but walking holy and sanctified is an intentional action in accordance with the Holy Spirit. So when we teach and don't disciple, we are failing to give the babies in Christ what they need to survive. We keep feeding them milk, when they should be ready for solid food. We must show new believers and those who have been slow to mature the way to walk with Christ. We must show them the difference between life and life more abundantly. Abundant life is walking in the power of Jesus Christ. We must teach them how to crucify the flesh, so that they might be resurrected into the power of Christ. The cost of discipleship must be understood in order to effectively know who and what the enemy is, so when the devil comes to steal, kill and destroy, we are confident in knowing his end (Revelation 20:10).

One example of discipleship as we see in the New Testament is Jesus and His disciples or followers. Jesus did not just teach them, they walked with Him studying His actions and His ways. To walk means the way we conduct ourselves or behave in a particular manner. Jesus modeled for the world what it meant to walk with God, commune with God and move in His power. His disciples followed Him after He called them and prepared them to go out into the world and make more disciples (Matthew 28:19). Discipleship is reaching people through people to show them the kingdom of God. It is a lifestyle, living each day with Jesus and for God. When we are in a situation of playing church, we can mistake church attendance for discipleship. We can also mistake being in a ministry serving that ministry, not Jesus for discipleship. In the real church of God, the body grows closer by reaching out to others together. When we go out to minister to or disciple others, the members of the body of Christ discover and hone their spiritual gifts. As we step out for God, making disciples as He commissioned, we teach by example, and glorify God to the world.

> Discipleship is reaching people through people to show the kingdom of God.

What Does the Real Church Look Like?

The church (the body of Christ) is the central purpose of God in this present age. It is an organism, not an organization. We have already established that it as one body of Christ with many members (such as you and I). We are called to be saints, sanctified in Christ Jesus (1 Corinth. 1:2). We have been redeemed and are saved through Jesus as the church of God. The body is endowed and empowered to do the service and the ministry of the church. "...the Spirit gives people their ministries in the church, including leadership ministry. The Spirit does so "as it wills" (1 Corinth. 12:11)."[2] So if the Spirit gives the people ministries to be of service in, then we will be successful as the Spirit leads and guides us in those ministries. Did the Lord endow you to work in the ministry you are serving in?

We must stay true to Christ and make Him central in all we do. This is the framework of the New Testament church – Jesus. This is also true for all activities the church participates in, which should be service and ministry to God. Each of these ministries or areas of service should be tied to scriptural activities that are fundamental to the kingdom of God being manifest here on earth as it is in heaven. If your fellowship with other believers is being led by the Spirit of the Lord in truth, you and the other believers will enjoy a time of peace, be strengthened and encouraged by the Holy Spirit, grow in numbers, and live in the fear of the Lord.

> The church is an organism, not an organization.

> Then had the churches rest throughout all Judaea and Galilee and Samaria, and were edified; and walking in the fear of the Lord, and in the comfort of the Holy Ghost, were multiplied (Acts 9:31).

Is this happening in your local fellowship as the church of the living God? Or is it operating like the local Elks Lodge? The church, as the body of Christ should offer so much more than group fellowship or 'club membership'. "There is the psychology of the group to be sure, and yet it is so much more; it is divine inter penetration. There is what the biblical writers call koinonia, deep inward fellowship in the power of the Spirit."[3]

Signs of Playing Church

If we now know what the real church of God looks like, let us divulge what some of the disorders of the church look like when the world has crept in. We can use the church at Corinth as an example:

But in giving this next instruction, I do not praise you, because when you meet together it is not for the better but for the worse. For, in the first place, when you meet together in church, I hear that there are divisions among you; and in part I believe it, for [doubtless] there have to be factions among you, so that those who are of approved character may be clearly recognized among you. So when you meet together, it is not to eat the Lord's Supper, for when you eat, each one hurries to get his own supper first [not waiting for others or the poor]. So one goes hungry while another gets drunk. What! Do you not have houses in which to eat and drink? Or do you show contempt for the church of God and humiliate those [impoverished believers] who have nothing? What will I say to you? Shall I praise you for this? In this I will not praise you! For I received from the Lord Himself that [instruction] which I passed on to you, that the Lord Jesus on the night in which He was betrayed took bread; and when He had given thanks, He broke it and said, "This is (represents) My body, which is [offered as a sacrifice] for you. Do this in [affectionate] remembrance of Me." In the same way, after supper He took the cup, saying, "This cup is the new covenant [ratified and established] in My blood; do this, as often as you drink it, in [affectionate] remembrance of Me." For every time you eat this bread and drink this cup, you are [symbolically] proclaiming [the fact of] the Lord's death until He comes [again]. So then whoever eats the bread or drinks the cup of the Lord in a way that is unworthy [of Him] will be guilty of [profaning and sinning against] the body and blood of the Lord. But a person must [prayerfully] examine himself [and his relationship to Christ], and only when he has done so should he eat of the bread and drink of the cup. For anyone who eats and drinks [without solemn reverence and heartfelt gratitude for the sacrifice of Christ], eats and drinks a judgment on himself if he does not recognize the body [of Christ]. That [careless and unworthy participation] is the reason why many among you are weak and sick, and a number sleep [in death]. But if we evaluated and judged ourselves honestly [recognizing our shortcomings and correcting our behavior], we would not be judged. But when we [fall short and] are judged by the Lord, we are disciplined [by undergoing His correction] so that we will not be condemned [to eternal punishment] along with the world. So then, my brothers and sisters, when you come together to eat [the Lord's Supper], wait for one another [and see to it that no one is left out]. If anyone is too hungry [to wait], let him eat at home, so that you will not come together for judgment [on yourselves]. About the remaining matters [of which I was informed], I will take care of them when I come. (1 Corinthians 11:17-34 AMP)

The Lord 's Supper is a time of remembrance in fellowship as the church of God. It is a holy time and we should be humbled as we remember the sacrifice Christ made for us on the cross. The bible says as often as you do this, do it in remembrance of Me. In the early church the Lord's Supper was a meal, unlike today. This church had distorted the sacrament, which every Christian was decreed to take at least once a year. This disorderly environment displayed at the church in Corinth was not of God, because God does things in decency and in order. We see the body of Christ at Corinth with divisions amongst them in verse 18, they have factions that show partiality in verse 19, and selfishness in verse 21. Further there is misuse of the church building and shaming (making those who have less feel bad) in verse 22, misconduct at the Lord's Supper in verses 27-30, and finally the lack of examination before taking the Lord's supper in verses 28-34. This conduct is fleshy and does not display the fruit of the Spirit. This behavior normally is unacceptable for the believers of God, but to carry on like this at a time that is supposed to be a time of worship, reverence and remembrance for the body of Christ is deplorable before God. God is not the author or confusion, and this is what was going on. We must make sure that we function as the real church and not in the dysfunctional behavior introduced by the enemy of our souls.

Identity Principle

We must learn to worship the Lord in a way that is not tied to religion or tradition, but in Spirit and in Truth.

The Grey Area

We have read what we need to do to make sure the body learns and walks as the true church, the temple of the Holy Spirit. We must look at ourselves in the light of Christ and move toward maturity. As we mature we can teach and disciple the new believers in Christ. When we do this we can function as the church biblically defined, and not be stuck in the dysfunctions of playing church, acting like the world.

As we grow we will learn by the teaching of the Holy Spirit how to truly worship the Lord. In this we see a necessity to teach the body of Christ how to worship the Lord, not tied to religion or tradition. Our fellowship time together is not a show, or an event. The times when the body comes together in fellowship to worship its head, Jesus Christ should be frequent. They should be sacred times of worship, praise and thanksgiving. These gatherings should be joyous times of testimony and encouragement. The church of God should take every opportunity to praise and worship together as believers. This could be a quick prayer at work with a co-worker. It could also be a word of encouragement as you pass your sister or brother in Christ during the day.

Foster provides us with seven steps into worship that I want to encourage you to use as you move from a religious posture to a posture of pure and undefiled worship to the Lord as His church.

Wanda L. Scott

Seven Simple Steps into Worship[4]

1. Practice the presence of God daily.
Try to pray continuously, punctuating every moment with inward praise, worship and adoration. Giving your full attention to Christ daily in bible study as His Holy Spirit teaches.

2. Have many different experiences of worship.
Worship God alone. In small groups not just for bible study, but in worship. These will empower and impact the larger Sunday gathering.

3. Find many ways to really prepare for the gathered experience of worship.
Prepare in such ways as going to bed early, inward examination and confession to God, reviewing scripture and hymn, as well as arriving early to prepare for worship.

4. Have a willingness to be gathered in the power of the Lord.
"as an individual I must learn to let go of my agenda, of my concern, of my being blessed, of my hearing the Word of God. The language of the gathered fellowship is not "I", but "we"."[5]

5. Cultivate holy dependency
Be utterly and completely dependent on God for anything to happen.

6. Absorb distractions with gratitude
Be willing to relax when things distract you, not getting upset but being able to dismiss it and re-center yourself on the Lord.

7. Learn to offer a sacrifice of worship
Worship God even when you don't feel like it. Worship is not about you or how you feel, but about the glory, mercy, faithfulness, and awesome presence of God.

Worshipping God in unity and oneness of Spirit opens up a marvelous opportunity to see the supernatural of God displayed through our gifts. Believers' gatherings are not to be mimicked or modeled after the world. We should expect God to be present by His Spirit, and for our very lives to be changed by His presence. The gifts of the Spirit function mightily when our worship is pure in spirit and in truth. God desires this time of communion with us as the body, in addition to our personal time with Him. The body is edified at the supernatural display of God, and grows to desire more of God's presence this way. We must foster and consistently have fellowship the way God designed and desires. Fellowship with worship, biblical edification and supernatural demonstration must be normal for the church of the living God. 'Playing church' must die, and pure and undefiled worship must thrive and flourish amongst believers in the body of Christ.

Wanda L. Scott

Jesus how might I worship you?
Teach me just what to do.

Show me how to come to you,
as your Church should do.

Clean us Lord, so we will be,
without spot or blemish;
Prepare us to be what you would want us to be.

Change me Lord
so You will come back for me.

WLS

POWER and PROMISE

DECLARATION: Repeat these out loud...and then answer the question.

1. ***I agree that I am the real church and that wherever I go Jesus Christ is represented.*** Do you exemplify Christ in your daily walk?

2. ***I agree that I have to stop 'playing' church in my walk with Jesus and grow so the universal church will thrive.*** Do you ever fellowship with other believers outside of your local church?

3. ***I agree that I am regened in Christ to resemble God and have His characteristics. My heredity has changed!*** Name (1) one way this changes your outlook about your inheritance in either your health or wealth.

Action for Abundant Life

AWARENESS: Do you believe that you are to make disciples? Is your life exemplified by love, obedience and the fruit of God's Spirit?

AWARENESS: How has not fully grasping the "cost of discipleship" caused you to be lax in your growth as a believer?

UNDERSTANDING: Which Identity Principle in this chapter did you relate to the most? Why?

AFTERWORD

IT IS MY PRAYER THAT THIS BOOK HAS BROUGHT A FIRE and an encouragement to your walk with Christ. The power of God by His Spirit is a necessity to grow in faith as a child of God. God's power is amazing. The unlimited power of God is the potential we begin to see as we move believing for MORE of God. This expectation is what will fuel our endurance to obtain the promises of God.

It is the hope of glory that ALL of God's children strive to grow in His grace and knowledge receiving everything He has predestined for us by faith.

Be diligent. Be determined. Be with the Lord in all you do.

It is the desire of God's heart to be with you and you with Him. AMEN.

Wanda L. Scott

Notes

Notes

Wanda L. Scott

Notes

Bibliography

ABUNDANT LIFE WITH JESUS
1. Youniss J.; McLellan J.A.; Yates M., , Volume 22, Number 2, April 1999, pp. 243-253(11), , Abstract

GOD'S POWER PERSONIFIED
1. Dietrich Bonhoeffer, *The Cost of Discipleship* (New York : Touchstone, 1995), p. 214
2. Richard Foster, *Celebration of Discipline* (New York : Harper Collins, 1998), p. 71
3. Foster, p. 71
4. Foster, p. 72
5. E. M. Bounds, *Power through Prayer* (Chicago : Moody Press, N.D.), p.38
6. Bounds, pp. 38,77
7. Foster, p. 33
8. Foster, p. 164
9. Foster, p. 164

How To Define Success
1. Charles Stanley, *Success God's Way* (Nashville : Thomas Nelson,), p. 26
2. Stanley, p. 24
3. Stanley, p. 22

GROWING BEYOND PLAYING CHURCH
1. Dietrich Bonhoeffer, *The Cost of Discipleship* (New York: Touchstone, 1995), p. 171
2. Cosgrove & Hatfield, *Church Conflicts* (Nashville : Abingdon, 1994), p. 16
3. Richard Foster, *Celebration of Discipline* (New York: Harper Collins, 1998), p. 164
4. Foster, pp. 170-172

Wanda L. Scott

Scripture References

LIFE WITH JESUS
John 10:10 (NRSV), p. 24 Ephesians 5:15-17 (NRSV), p. 25 Joshua 1:8 (KJV), p. 25 Matthew 26:41 (KJV), p. 27 2 Corinthians 6:14, p. 27 Exodus 34:12-16 (KJV), p. 27 1 John 2:15-17 (NRSV), p. 28 1 Corinthians 10:24, p. 28 Genesis 6:5, p. 29 Revelations 12:7, p. 29

SOMETHING ABOUT THAT NAME
Acts 4:18 (NRSV), p. 96 Habakkuk 2:14, p. 97 Acts 2:38 (KJV), p. 97 Mark 16:17-18 (NKJV), p. 97 John 14:26 (KJV), p. 98 Revelations 12, p. 98 1 Corinthians 10:4, p. 98 Luke 21:8 (KJV), p. 99 John 15:16 (KJV), p. 99 John 15:4-8 (NKJV), p. 99 Romans 7:4-5 (NJV), p. 99 Galatians 5:22, p. 100 Matthew 28: 16-20, p. 100 Matthew 7:15-20 (NKJV), p. 101 John 16:23-24 (KJV), p. 101 John 16:26 (KJV), p. 101 John 14:13-14 (KJV), p. 102 1 Peter 1:4-9 (KJV), p. 103 Ecclesiastes 3:1, p. 103 1 Corinthians 10:13, p. 103 Romans 9:22-23 (NKJV), p. 103 James 1:17 (NKJV), p. 104 James 1:6-8, p. 104 Philippians 3:12-14, p. 105

GOD'S POWER PERSONIFIED
Proverbs 24:5 (NRSV), p. 32 Hosea 4:6 (KJV), p. 33 Matthew 28:16-20 (NKJV), p. 33 Romans 6:16, p. 34 Hebrews 11:6 (NRSV), p. 34 Matthew 13:11, p. 35 Matthew 6:9, p. 35 Acts 16:25-31 (KJV), p. 36 Mark 11:24, p. 36 Acts 6:4, p. 37 Matthew 5:44 (KJV), p. 37 Jeremiah 3:15 (NKJV), p. 37 Mark 11:17, p. 38 Philippians 3:15, p. 38 Matthew 18:20, p. 38 Hebrews 10:25, p. 38 Proverbs 1:7 (NRSV), p. 39 Isaiah 55:9, p. 39 Proverbs 5:23 (NKJV), p. 40 Habakkuk 2:14 (KJV), p.41

HOW TO DEFINE SUCCESS
Joshua 1:7-8 (KJV), p. 43 Ephesians 2:10, p. 43 Proverbs 16:3 (KJV), p. 44 1 Corinthians 6:12 (NRSV), p. 44 Isaiah 48:17-18 (KJV), p. 44 Isaiah 45:2, p. 44 Deuteronomy 10:12-13 (KJV), p. 45 Romans 8:28, p. 48 1 Samuel 16:7, p. 48 Romans 12:2 (NRSV), p. 49 John 13:35, p. 50

GROWING BEYOND PLAYING CHURCH
Ephesians 4:15-16 (NKJV), p. 71 2 Corinthians 3:18 (NKJV), p. 73 Titus 3:3-7 (NRSV), p. 73 1 Corinthians 4:6, p. 73 Ephesians 4:7, 11-14 (NKJV), p. 75 1 Corinthians 12, p. 75 Romans 11:29, p. 75 Revelation 20:10, p. 77 Matthew 28:19, p. 77 1 Corinthians 1:2, p. 78 1 Corinthians 12:11, p. 78 Acts 9:31 (KJV), p. 78 1 Corinthians 11:17-34 (NKJV), p. 80

Are you ready to be Encouraged, Empowered and Educated?

Wanda L. Scott is a Speaker, Educator, Author and Consultant who *Encourages Faith*, *Empowers Relationships*, and *Educates others for Abundant Life*!

Rev. Wanda L. Scott has been captivating audiences for over 10 years. Invite Rev. Wanda to come deliver a powerful Word that *teaches the Power of a personal relationship with Jesus Christ, how to prioritizing Love in every Relationship,* as she expounds on the Word of God educating you on "Agreement" for life in the Kingdom of God!

Visit www.WandaLScott.com *to Book Wanda and to view & purchase ALL of her ministry resources*.

Connect with us:
 @WandasWalk

 Facebook.com/AuthorWandaLScott

OTHER BOOKS BY WANDA L. SCOTT

Life and Love

We all need love as we go through this life. We find that never failing, always giving love in the Lord as He grants us new life by His Sprit!

In her latest publication Life and Love, Wanda L. Scott takes a very real look at the choices we make in the *grey areas* of our lives. **This first book in the *Identity for Life Series*** lays out for us the scripture that feeds us the fundamentals of our Christ identity.

- Each book gives Identity Principles and shows us how the word of God applies to our everyday living walking in love toward God and others.
- There is a specific focus on agreement with God's Word and how that lays the foundation for personal accountability and our responsibility to those we come in contact with every day.

When we do this we walk as witnesses who have received the love, grace and forgiveness of God through Christ Jesus.

WHAT IS THE GREY AREA?
On the path of life are these grey areas which can be filled with people, opportunities, obstacles, circumstances, and choices. It is in this grey area that one can find God and change his/her final destination. It is in this grey area that one can agree with God and make choices that help them find "purpose", "peace", "prosperity", and "abundant life" in Jesus Christ.

To learn more about Wanda's workshops, teachings, and other resources visit her on the Web at: www.wandalscott.com

Or write:
                      Wanda L. Scott
                      P.O. Box 120804
                      Nashville, TN 37212-0804

"I" Can Relate
How Not To Lose Yourself in Relationships

How Are You Doing In Relationships?

The "**SHIP**" in relationship can take you down traitorous waters that can have your life turning up-side down with every high wave, flowing in the wrong direction with every misguided emotion, and heading toward a shipwreck that your heart can't stand again.

R E L A T I O N S H "I" P

- Am I "RE"peating patterns in Relationships?
- What is my response based "ON"?
- Do I know where this relation"SHIP" is heading?

God is a God of relationship, and He says in His word that He is love. Using the wisdom in the word of God, we will see how the Lord can guide us in having more love in our relationships.

To learn more about Wanda's workshops, teachings, and other resources visit her on the Web at: www.wandalscott.com

Or write:

Wanda L. Scott
P.O. Box 120804
Nashville, TN 37212-0804

Wanda L. Scott

Where are you in life's relationships?

What have you been through in your lifetime?

"A good poet is hard to find and welcome when she finds us. Let us welcome Wanda Scott to the family of poets." *Nikki Giovanni*

A Lifetime of Relationships: Letters, Poems and Words of Love is an evolution and exploration into the life of Wanda L. Scott, a journey through the tumultuous emotions of life's experiences. It is a compilation of passionate poetry reflecting on life and love, pain and powerlessness, highs and lows. This book touches you where you are in life's relationships. It will help others to reflect on their life and inquire how they can express themselves to release life's emotions.

Life has a unique way of entangling us in the midst of our relationships and emotions. Are you ready to move through life releasing instead of storing up the pain? How do you express yourself in these emotional times? How do you move past the emotional pain to spiritual healing, true love, and peace? One way is to express ourselves with letters, poems and words of love.

A Lifetime of Relationships is a vehicle to demonstrate God's power of creative expression through his children, and has a **companion workshop** that stresses *God's Word on Godly Relationships*.

To learn more about Wanda's workshops, teachings, and other resources visit her on the Web at: www.wandalscott.com

Or write:

Wanda L. Scott
P.O. Box 120804
Nashville, TN 37212-0804

POWER and PROMISE

www.ingramcontent.com/pod-product-compliance
Lightning Source LLC
Chambersburg PA
CBHW032058150426
43194CB00006B/566